D1318787

STRIPES, STRIPES, STRIPES
Knits with Color and Texture

Sandy Scoville

Martingale®
& COMPANY

Stripes, Stripes, Stripes: Knits with Color and Texture
© 2008 by Sandy Scoville

Martingale & Company®
20205 144th Ave. NE
Woodinville, WA 98072-8478 USA
www.martingale-pub.com

Printed in China
13 12 11 10 09 08   8 7 6 5 4 3 2 1

Library of Congress Cataloging-in-Publication Data
Library of Congress Control Number 2007041225

ISBN: 978-1-56477-797-3

CREDITS

President & CEO: Tom Wierzbicki
Publisher: Jane Hamada
Editorial Director: Mary V. Green
Managing Editor: Tina Cook
Technical Editor: Donna Druchunas
Copy Editor: Liz McGehee
Design Director: Stan Green
Assistant Design Director: Regina Girard
Illustrator: Adrienne Smitke
Cover & Text Designer: Stan Green
Photographer: Brent Kane

MISSION STATEMENT

Dedicated to providing quality products and service to inspire creativity.

CONTENTS

INTRODUCTION

My dictionary describes the word _stripes_ as long narrow strips or bands that differ from others. There's no reference to color, which is the first visual thought that most often comes to mind when you hear the word.

I prefer to think of stripes in terms of pattern and texture. Only then do I translate this mental picture into color. A perfect example of this is the stylish White-on-White Elegance Afghan on page 11. I've combined every uniquely textured white and off-white yarn I could find into patterned stripes.

Choosing colors is another challenge. Palettes pleasing to one knitter may not inspire another. Since yarns are now available in breathtakingly gorgeous colors, the possibilities are endless. So, in most projects, you'll find suggestions for alternate colorways—hopefully leading to your own interpretations.

Colors often invoke mental images and thoughts simply by their expression. Think blue, for instance. Blue sky? Blue Monday? Baby boy? Now, mentally change "blue" to "navy." What do you visualize? I see jeans and harbor scenes dressed in red, white, and blue. Must be my San Diego ties.

This book is divided into sections that express related thoughts and images in color. After all, "It's Not Always Black or White." So, look for a Touch of Color Afghan in that section. If you try hard enough, you might detect the aroma of your favorite blend as you knit with the warm browns, peaches, and lavenders featured in "Tea or Coffee?" Then, move on to the deeper "Jewel Box" tones in the Bed of Roses and Spring Ribbons afghans. Turn to the "Hot and Spicy" pages for the Desert Heat Afghan and Chili Peppers Hat and Scarf. And finally, relax with the "Soft and Sweet" pastels of the Sunshine Pillows, Romantic Ripple Vest, and Pistachio Shell. These, and other projects not mentioned here, make up my _Stripes, Stripes, Stripes_.

Ultimately, I think of stripes as the "colorful" texture in the events of my life. Thank you for sharing this stripe-filled experience with me.

—Sandy

HELPFUL INFORMATION

Following are some suggestions for working with stripes, color, and texture intended to assist you in knitting the patterns in this book. It is my hope that you will have fun while creating projects that become uniquely yours.

CHOOSING YARNS

When you can't find the yarn specified in a pattern at your local yarn store or Internet retailer, don't despair. Substituting another yarn is fairly straightforward if you keep a few simple guidelines in mind.

Yarn Weights

The yarns used in this book were chosen almost entirely from the collections of three of my favorite suppliers and are widely available throughout the United States. Many of them are also available internationally. I've chosen them for the quality of fiber content and for the gorgeous range of colors available. You can find a listing of to these companies on page 79.

There are many other fine yarns on the market today. Because of the abundance of choice, it is impossible for any one store to carry all yarns. For that reason, the yarns listed in each pattern are followed by a code that is becoming standard on many yarn labels and in most U.S. pattern books. For example, an icon with the number 4 on a yarn label or within a pattern means that the referenced yarn is considered by the manufacturer or the designer to be worsted weight. You can find a chart defining all yarn-weight codes on page 5. The chart also suggests needle sizes and stitch gauges that are appropriate for the yarn weight.

STANDARD YARN-WEIGHT SYSTEM

Yarn-Weight Symbol and Category Names	1 Super Fine	2 Fine	3 Light	4 Medium	5 Bulky	6 Super Bulky
Types of Yarns in Category	Sock, Fingering, Baby	Sport, Baby	DK, Light Worsted	Worsted, Afghan, Aran	Chunky, Craft, Rug	Bulky, Roving
Knit Gauge Ranges in Stockinette Stitch to 4"	27 to 32 sts	23 to 26 sts	21 to 24 sts	16 to 20 sts	12 to 15 sts	6 to 11 sts
Recommended Needle in Metric Size Range	2.25 to 3.25 mm	3.25 to 3.75 mm	3.75 to 4.5 mm	4.5 to 5.5 mm	5.5 to 8 mm	8 mm and larger
Recommended Needle in U.S. Size Range	1 to 3	3 to 5	5 to 7	7 to 9	9 to 11	11 and larger

Texture

Ideally, using this chart, you should be able to substitute any worsted-weight yarn. Please keep in mind, however, the code is intended as a guide only. The term "weight" is best considered to be a reference to stitch gauge, *not* ounces or grams.

There are other factors that will affect the look and feel of your finished project. Consider texture. A bulky, brushed mohair-type yarn will knit much differently than a bulky yarn suitable for some afghans, place mats, rugs, etc. These yarns may all carry the same code and work to the same stitch gauge, but the knitting results will be quite different.

Color

Combining colors for knitting projects depends on what yarns are available to you. Some of the large projects in this book use a multitude of colors. Don't limit your selections by trying to match them. Instead, let personal choice dictate your purchases. Alternate colorways are suggested throughout the book to encourage you to personalize your knitting.

For example, instead of using several pastel colors in an afghan, using only two might result in the perfect throw for your favorite chair. How about using only black and white for sophistication, brown and cream to suggest warmth, or blue and green for a nautical look? Change jewel tones to pastels. What if you used a self-striping yarn throughout (see page 6)?

Before you buy yarn, ask your retailer if you can exchange colors. If not, consider purchasing only one skein of each color choice in order to make a sample swatch in the pattern stitch you will be using. Often the colors look great on the skein, but may surprise you when actually knit in pattern.

KNITTING WITH MULTIPLE COLORS

There are many different techniques for knitting with multiple colors. In this section, I describe those that I find easiest and most useful.

Changing Colors and Carrying Yarns

Many knitting books suggest using bobbins when working with small sections of different colors. I dislike using bobbins, so I recommend them only when they seem absolutely necessary. Those dangling bits of plastic wrapped with yarn drive me nuts! They tend to end up on the wrong side of my work and tangle just as much as when knitting multiple strands directly from the skeins. This is a personal choice. If you prefer using bobbins, please do so. I prefer to use a separate skein of yarn for each color.

Suggestions are made in several patterns as to whether to carry yarns or cut the strands after each use. This is dependent on several things. Bulky-weight yarns may not always carry well, because they can add bulk in the wrong places. Some afghans might not have borders, so yarns should be cut after each use. For afghans, try carrying the main color and cutting and rejoining others as you go.

Using Self-Striping Yarns

So you've decided, to heck with changing colors. There are so many yummy self-striping yarns available, why not use one of them instead? Great idea! Maybe.

If you are making an afghan, there may not be an issue. But when knitting garments, consider where the stripes will appear. Will they be wide or narrow? As you knit, will they fall where you want them to?

Working a small sample swatch will not answer these questions, because the swatch will be narrower than your finished project. If possible, knit an entire skein in the width of your project. Be sure to carefully rip out the swatch to reclaim the yarn.

Always think ahead. Are all pieces the same width? Horizontal stripes on a cardigan will be of different height on the two front pieces than on the wider back piece. Some self-striping yarns are "striated," meaning the color changes are gradual and provide a more subtle color change. Each shade blends into the next. These striated yarns add interest to garments and provide a unique look to each project.

Vertical stripes usually offer more of a challenge than horizontal stripes. The Stripes the Easy Way vest on page 25 uses a striated yarn. The simple pattern was designed for your first attempt at using vertical stripes. The pattern instructions tell you how to ensure that the stripes will appear matched as you add new skeins and work the fronts.

To add new skeins on any project where a color change is not indicated, pull out the new strand to the place where the color on the strand matches the last color knit. Cut here and begin to knit with the new strand. Save the cut length to sew seams, make I-cord, or add edgings. Always add new skeins at the beginning of a row or round.

ALL THOSE PESKY TAILS!

Yikes! OK, now that the whining is out of the way, here's how to make this necessary finishing chore pleasant. Choose a time when you are with family or friends or watching a movie on TV. Unlike following a pattern, weaving in tails is a mindless task. Weave while you visit.

For afghans, promise a friend another cookie if she helps. Have her sit with you side by side and begin at opposite ends. See who can reach the center first! Before you know it, the work will be finished. Just kidding! But do accept her help if she offers.

Begin by threading a tail into a tapestry or yarn needle. If there are seams, weave into the seam about 1½" in one direction, then turn and weave back, catching the other strand to hold it in place. A tail that is woven this way will usually not pull out. If there are no seams, carefully weave in the same manner through a matching color.

To weave in the tails as you knit, I suggest weaving only one tail and leaving the other to be woven in later. It may be possible to work over both strands—but only if using a very thin yarn. Try it and check how it looks on the right side of your work. When working over only one tail, use the one that matches the last color used. It will blend well and not show on the right side.

When you join a new color, leave a 3 to 4" tail on both the old and the new yarns. Knit two stitches with the new yarn normally, then pull the tails of both yarns down over the front of the working yarn as you make the next stitch. On the next stitch, lift the tails up behind the working yarn and knit the next stitch normally. Keep alternating in this way until the tails are completely worked in.

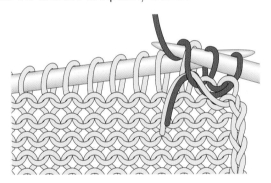

Weave tails on the wrong side as you knit.

FRINGE

Cut strands of yarn twice the desired finished length of fringe. Fold fringe in half and insert crochet hook in stitch from back to front. Catch folded fringe and pull through knitted piece, creating a loop. Draw fringe ends through loop and pull to tighten. Trim, as necessary, to even lengths.

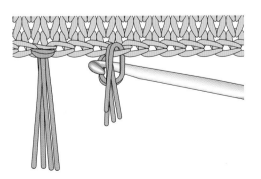

SEWING SEAMS

In the project instructions, I've indicated the types of seams I used to finish the projects. If you are unfamiliar with the seaming techniques I mentioned, check in any knitting encyclopedia or ask for help at your local yarn shop. If you know other types of seams and prefer to use those, that is perfectly acceptable. Just be sure that you match up the stripes on the different pieces as you sew them together. The goal is to have neat seams that make the garment look handmade but not homemade.

METRIC CONVERSIONS

m	=	yds	x	0.9144
yds	=	m	x	1.0936
g	=	oz	x	28.35
oz	=	g	x	0.0352

ABBREVIATIONS

beg.................begin(ning)
BO ....bind off
ch(s) ....chain
CO ....cast on
cont...............continue, continuing
dec................decrease, decreasing
dpn(s) ....double-pointed needle(s)
inc................increase, increasing
g....................gram
K ....knit
K1b ....knit next stitch in row below
K1f&b............knit 1 stitch through front loop and 1 stitch through back loop of same stitch
K2tog............knit 2 stitches together
K2tog tbl........knit 2 stitches together through back loops
kw ....knitwise
LH.................left hand
M1 ....make one stitch
m...................meter(s)
MC................main color
mm...............millimeter(s)
oz.................ounce(s)
P....................purl
P2tog.............purl 2 stitches together

P2tog tbl........purl 2 stitches together through back loops
patt................pattern
pm................place marker
psso..............pass slipped stitch over
PU.................pick up and knit
pw.................purlwise
rem...............remain(ing)
rep................repeat(ing)
RH.................right hand
RS.................right side
sl ....slip
sm ....slip marker
st(s)...............stitch(es)
St st ....stockinette stitch: knit on RS rows, purl on WS rows
tbl.................through back loop
tog................together
WS ....wrong side
wyib..............with yarn in back
wyif...............with yarn in front
yb.................yarn back
yd(s) ....yard(s)
yf...................yarn forward
YO................yarn over

IT'S NOT ALWAYS BLACK OR WHITE

Texture defines this luxurious throw and satisfies on so many levels! Fairly easy to knit, it's designed to use almost any yarn. By keeping the stripes narrow, variations in yarn weight simply add to the textured look. For this throw, I chose shades of white and off-white. I used two skeins (about 50 grams each) of 10 different yarns and one carry-along yarn. I then added a basic worsted-weight wool for the connecting stripes.

Skill Level: Intermediate
Size: 48" x 64"

MATERIALS

Yarns used in the model are from Crystal Palace Yarns and Plymouth Yarn Company in various weights and shades of white. Since it's unlikely that you will find all of the specialty yarns listed below at your local yarn shop, feel free to substitute yarns of similar texture and weight.

CRYSTAL PALACE YARNS

A   2 skeins of Nubbles (90% wool, 10% nylon; 29 yds; 50 g), color 201 (5)

B   2 skeins of Shimmer (86% acrylic, 14% nylon; 90 yds; 50 g), color 1736 (4)

C   2 skeins of BeBop (100% nylon; 64 yds; 50 g), color 200 (4)

D   2 skeins of Rave (100% nylon; 44 yds; 50 g), color 300 (5)

E   2 skeins of Party (100% nylon; 87 yds; 50 g), color 200 (5)

F   1 skein of Splash (100% polyester; 94 yds; 100 g), color 201 (5)

G   2 skeins of Musique (45% acrylic, 40% wool, 15% cotton; 65 yds; 50 g), color 204 (5)

H   2 skeins of Deco-Ribbon (70% acrylic, 30% nylon; 80 yds; 50 g), color 300 (5)

I   1 skein of Mikado Ribbon (50% cotton, 50% viscose; 112 yds; 50 g), color 1806 (4) *

J   1 skein of Fling (95% nylon, 5% metallic fiber; 130 yds; 50 g), color 3687*

*Yarns I and J are always used together as one yarn. I is a ribbon yarn and J is a carry-along metallic yarn.

PLYMOUTH YARN CO. YARNS

K   2 skeins of Stars from Adriafil (50% viscose, 50% nylon; 65m, 71 yds; 50 g), color 80 (4)

MC 5 skeins of Galway from Plymouth Yarn Co. (100% wool; 210 yds; 100 g), color 8 (4)

• Size 9 (5.5 mm) circular needle, at least 29" long, or size to obtain gauge

• Tapestry needle

GAUGE

18 sts and 24 rows = 4" in St st with MC

DIRECTIONS

This afghan is <u>worked in one piece, with the colors and stitch patterns changing for each stripe.</u> There are 17 sections: 9 main stripes and 8 narrow row stripe sections. See the diagram on page 13 for the arrangement of the stripes.

Note: For this project, I cut the yarn after each use. For tips on working with stripes with different yarns, see "Changing Colors and Carrying Yarns" on page 5 and decide which technique works best for you.

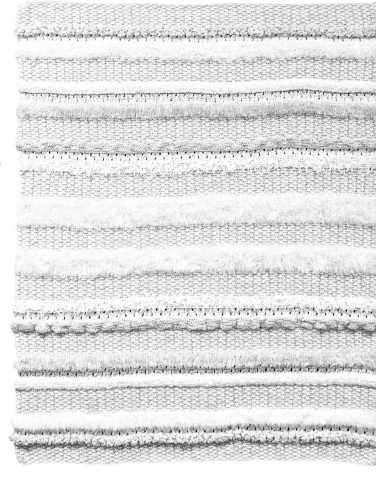

Stripe 1: Main-Stripe Section

With MC, CO 217 sts.

Row 1 (RS): Cont with MC, K2, *P3, K2, rep from * across.

Row 2: Purl.

Row 3: P3, *K2, P3, rep from * to last 4 sts, K2, P2.

Row 4: Purl.

Rows 5–24: Rep rows 1–4 another 5 times.

Stripe 2: Narrow-Stripes Section

Row 1 (RS): With A, purl.

Row 2: With A, knit.

Rows 3 and 4: With A, rep rows 1 and 2.

Rows 5–7: With B, knit.

Rows 8, 10, 12, 14: With B, purl.

Row 9: With B, K3, K2tog, *YO, K3, K2tog, rep from * to last 2 sts, K2—216 sts.

Row 11: Knit.

Row 13: With B, K4, K2tog, *YO, K3, K2tog, rep from * to last 5 sts, K5—215 sts.

Rows 15 and 16: With B, knit.

Rows 17–26: With C, knit.

Stripes 3, 5, 7, 9, 11, 13, 15: Main Stripe Sections

Row 1 (RS): With MC, K1f&b, knit to last 2 sts, K1f&b, K1—217 sts.

Row 2: Cont with MC, purl.

Rows 3–26: Rep rows 1–24 of main stripe.

Stripe 4: Narrow-Stripes Section

Row 1 (RS): With D, knit.

Row 2: With D, knit.

Row 3: With D, purl.

Rows 4–7: With D, rep rows 2 and 3.

Row 8: With D, knit.

Rows 9–20: With E, rep rows 5–16 of stripe 2.

Rows 21–30: With F, rep rows 17–26 of stripe 2.

Stripe 6: Narrow-Stripes Section

With G, H, and I/J (held tog) instead of D, E, and F, rep rows 1–30 of stripe 4.

Stripes 8 and 10: Center-Stripe Sections

Rows 1 (RS) and 2: With K, knit.

Row 3: With K, purl.

Row 4: With K, knit.

Rows 5–12: With K, rep rows 3 and 4.

Note: You have completed the center sections of the throw. The remaining sections are now worked in reverse order.

Stripe 12: Narrow-Stripes Section

Rows 1 (RS)–10: With I and J held tog, knit.

Rows 11–22: With H, rep rows 5–16 of stripe 2.

Rows 23 and 24: With G, knit.

Row 25: With G, purl.

Row 26: With G, knit.

Rows 27–30: With G, rep rows 25 and 26 twice.

Stripe 14: Narrow-Stripes Section

With F, E, and D, rep rows 1–30 of stripe 12.

Stripe 16: Narrow-Stripes Section

Rows 1–22: With C and B, work rows 1–22 of stripe 12.

Row 23: With A, purl.

Row 24: With A, knit.

Rows 25 and 26: Rep rows 23 and 24.

Stripe 17: Main-Stripe Section

Work as for stripe 3 through row 25.
BO all sts. Weave in ends.

48"	
Stripe 17: main stripe	MC
Stripe 16: narrow stripes	C, B, A
Stripe 15: main stripe	MC
Stripe 14: narrow stripes	F, E, D
Stripe 13: main stripe	MC
Stripe 12: narrow stripes	I/J, H, G
Stripe 11: main stripe	MC
Stripe 10: center stripe	K
Stripe 9: main stripe	MC
Stripe 8: center stripe	K
Stripe 7: main stripe	MC
Stripe 6: narrow stripes	G, H, I/J
Stripe 5: main stripe	MC
Stripe 4: narrow stripes	D, E, F
Stripe 3: main stripe	MC
Stripe 2: narrow stripes	A, B, C
Stripe 1: main stripe	MC

64"

FANCY RIB TEE

Here's the perfect tee to wear with your favorite black or white slacks. No boring ribbing for this top. The crossover rib stitch is easy to knit and adds interest.

Skill Level: Easy/Intermediate
Sizes: Small (Medium, Large)
Finished Bust: 34 (38, 42)"

MATERIALS

Dolly from Cascade Yarns (100% merino wool; 153 yds, 140 m; 1.76 oz, 50 g) in following amounts and colors: 🔳
  A   5 (6, 7) skeins of color 1 (white)
  B   3 (4, 5) skeins of color 330 (charcoal gray)
• Size 5 (3.75 mm) needles or size to obtain gauge
• Tapestry needle

GAUGE

24 sts and 32 rows = 4" in St st with MC

BACK AND FRONT (Make 2 identical pieces)

To reduce the number of yarn tails to weave in, carry A along the side edge to the first row of the center ribbing, then carry B along the side edge to the top section. Cut the contrasting color used for each narrow stripe and continue working with the background color.

Lower Ribbing

With A, CO 103 (115, 127) sts.

Row 1 (RS): P1, *K2, P1, rep from * across.

Row 2: K1, *YO, K2, pass YO over both sts, K1, rep from * across.

Rows 3–14 (18, 18): Rep rows 1 and 2 another 6 (8, 8) times.

Body

Row 1 (RS): Cont with A, K1f&b, knit to last 2 sts, K1f&b, K1—105 (117, 129) sts.

Row 2: Purl.

Rows 3–10 (18, 18): With A, work in St st.

BEGIN PATTERN:

Row 1 (RS): With B, K 7 (6, 3), (sl 2 pw wyib, K6) 11 (13, 15) times, sl 2 pw wyib, K8 (5, 4).

Row 2: With B, K8 (5, 4), (sl 2 pw wyif, K6) 11 (13, 15) times, sl 2 pw wyif, K7 (6, 3).

TRY THIS!

Stitches can be difficult to see in stark black. Use a charcoal gray yarn instead of black. There are just enough light fibers to allow for distinct pattern texture and make the stitches easier to see. Also, try switching the two colors in the pattern for an entirely different look.

Rows 3–10: With A, work in St st.

Rows 11 and 12: Rep rows 1 and 2.

Rows 13–18: With A, work in St st.

Rows 19 and 20: Rep rows 1 and 2.

Rows 21–24: With A, work in St st.

Rows 25 and 26: Rep rows 1 and 2.

Rows 27 and 28: With A, work in St st.

Waist Ribbing

Row 1 (RS): With B, K1, *P1, K1, rep from * across.

Row 2: With B, P1, *K1, P1, rep from * across.

Rows 3–6 (8, 8): Rep rows 1 and 2.

Row 7 (9, 9): With B, K1, *P3, K1, rep from * across.

Row 8 (10, 10): With B, P1, *K3, P1, rep from * across.

Next 6 (8, 8) rows: Work last 2 rows another 3 (4, 4) times.

Next 6 (8, 8) rows: Rep rows 1 and 2 another 3 (4, 4) times.

Top Section

Row 1 (RS): With A, K7 (6, 3), (sl 2 pw wyib, K6) 11 (13, 15) times, sl 2 pw wyib, K8 (5, 4).

Row 2: With A, K8 (5, 4), (sl 2 pw wyif, K6) 11 (13, 15) times, sl 2 pw wyif, K7 (6, 3).

Rows 3–6: With B, work in St st.

Rows 7 and 8: Rep rows 1 and 2.

Rows 9–14: With B, work in St st.

Rows 15 and 16: Rep rows 1 and 2.

Rows 17–24: With B, work in St st.

Rows 25 and 26: Rep rows 1 and 2.

SHAPE ARMHOLES:

Row 27 (RS): With A, BO 6 sts for underarm; cut A; with B, knit across—99 (111, 123) sts.

Row 28: With B, BO 6 sts for underarm, purl across—93 (105, 117) sts.

Rows 29–36: With B, work in St st. Rejoin A.

Rows 37 and 38: With A, work in St st.

Row 39: With B, K10 (8, 6), (sl 2 pw wyib, K6) 9 (11, 13) times, sl 2 pw wyib, K9 (7, 5).

Row 40: With B, K9 (7, 5), (sl 2 pw wyif, K6) 9 (11, 13) times, sl 2 pw wyif, K10 (8, 6).

Rows 41–44: With A, work in St st.

Rows 45 and 46: Rep rows 39 and 40.

Rows 47–52: With A, work in St st.

Rows 53 and 54: Rep rows 39 and 40.

Rows 55–62: With A, work in St st.

Rows 63 and 64: Rep rows 39 and 40. Cut B.

Rows 65–74: With A, work in St st.

Boat-Neck Ribbing

Row 1 (RS): P1, K1f&b, P1, *K2, P1, rep from * across—94 (106, 118) sts.

Row 2: K1, *YO, K2, pass YO over both sts, K1, rep from * across.

Row 3: P1, *K2, P1, rep from * across.

Row 4: K1, *YO, K2, pass YO over both sts, K1, rep from * across.

Rows 5–10 (14, 14): Rep rows 3 and 4 another 3 (5, 5) times.

BO in ribbing. Sew shoulder seams in about 3 (3, 3½)" from armhole edges.

SLEEVES

Hold one side edge with RS facing you; with A, PU 88 (94, 94) sts along edge of armhole. Carry A along side edge; cut B after each use.

Row 1 (WS): With A, purl.

Row 2 (RS): With A, knit.

Row 3: With A, purl.

Rows 4–9: Rep rows 2 and 3.

Row 10: With B, K3 (2, 2), sl 2 pw wyib, (K6, sl 2 pw wyib) 10 (11, 11) times, K3 (2, 2).

Row 11: With B, K3 (2, 2), sl 2 pw wyif, (K6, sl 2 pw wyif), 10 (11, 11) times, K3 (2, 2).

Rows 12 and 13: With A, rep rows 2 and 3.

Row 14: With A, K1, K2tog tbl, knit to last 3 sts, K2tog, K1—86 (92, 92) sts.

Row 15: Purl.

Rows 16–19: With A, rep rows 2 and 3.

Row 20: With B, K2 (1, 1), sl 2 pw wyib, (K6, sl 2 pw wyib) 10 (11, 11) times, K2 (1, 1).

Row 21: With B, purl.

Rows 22–25: With A, rep rows 2 and 3.

Rows 26 and 27: With A, rep rows 14 and 15—84 (90, 90) sts.

Row 28: With B, K9 (8, 8), sl 2 pw wyib, (K6, sl 2 pw wyib) 8 (9, 9) times, K9 (8, 8).

Row 29: With B, K9 (8, 8), sl 2 pw wyif, (K6, sl 2 pw wyif) 8 (9, 9) times, K9 (8, 8).

Rows 30 and 31: With A, rep rows 2 and 3.

Rows 32 and 33: With A, rep rows 14 and 15—82 (88, 88) sts.

Row 34: With B, K8 (7, 7), sl 2 pw wyib, (K6, sl 2 pw wyib) 8 (9, 9) times, K8 (7, 7).

Row 35: With B, K8 (7, 7), sl 2 pw wyif, (K6, sl 2 pw wyif) 8 (9, 9) times, K8 (7, 7).

Rows 36 and 37: With A, rep rows 2 and 3.

Rows 38 and 39: With B, rep rows 34 and 35.

Rows 40–43: With A, rep rows 2 and 3.

Rows 44 and 45: With A, rep rows 14 and 15—80 (86, 86) sts.

Rows 46 and 47 (46–51, 46–51): With A, rep rows 2 and 3 another 1 (3, 3) times.

Last row: With A, K1, K2tog tbl, knit across—79 (85, 85) sts.

SLEEVE RIBBING:

Rows 1–10: Rep rows 1 and 2 of lower ribbing.

BO in ribbing.

Work second sleeve in same manner.

FINISHING

Sew underarm and side seams, carefully matching stripes.

Weave in ends.

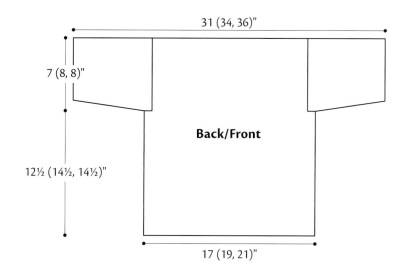

A TOUCH OF COLOR AFGHAN

Color can set a mood in your room. In the photographed model, cool hues of neutral browns and beiges are striped with an added splash of warm teal and copper—perfect for southwestern desert dwellers. Choose warmer shades of browns and tans to suggest a cozy feeling in a midwestern home.

Skill Level: Advanced
Size: Approx 50" x 60"

MATERIALS

220 Superwash from Cascade Yarns (100% Superwash wool; 220 yds; 3.5 oz, 100 g) in following amounts and colors: (**4**)

A	3 skeins of color 817 (off-white)	
B	4 skeins of color 873 (beige)	
C	4 skeins of color 815 (black)	
D	2 skeins of color 875 (taupe)	
E	1 skein of color 876 (copper)	

Galway from Plymouth Yarn Co. (100% wool; 210 yds; 100 g)

F	1 skein of color 139 (turquoise)	

- Size 8 (5 mm) needles or size to obtain gauge
- Size 8 (5 mm) circular needle, at least 29" long (for edging)
- Tapestry needle

TRY THIS!
Look around your room and choose one or two colors from a piece of art or fabric that bring you joy. Substitute these colors for E and F to make the afghan uniquely yours.

GAUGE

Note: The sections of this afghan are knit with different pattern stitches, each of which has a slightly different gauge.

18 sts and 24 rows = 4" in St st

Note: This throw is knit in eight panels and sewn together to create the offset stripe pattern. To keep track of color changes, check or cross off each stripe in the diagram on page 22 as you complete it. Also, for this project, I cut the yarn after each use. For tips on working with stripes in different yarns, see "Changing Colors and Carrying Yarns" on page 5 and decide which technique works best for you.

RIGHT SIDE PANEL

With A, CO 32 sts.

Row 1 (RS): P1, K6, (P6, K6) twice, P1.

Row 2: K1, P6, (K6, P6) twice, K1.

Rows 3–10: Rep rows 1 and 2.

Row 11: P7, (K6, P6) twice, P1.

Row 12: K7, (P6, K6) twice, K1.

Rows 13–20: Rep rows 11 and 12. Change to B.

Row 21: With B, knit.

Rows 22–40: Cont with B, rep rows 2–20. Change to A.

Row 41: With A, knit.

Rows 42–60: Cont with A, rep rows 2–20. Change to B.

Row 61: With B, knit.

Rows 62–80: Cont with B, rep rows 2–20. Change to C.

Row 81: With C, knit.

Rows 82–100: Cont with C, rep rows 2–20. Change to B.

Cont in patt, always working a knit row at the beg of each color change. Change colors every 20 rows in the following sequence: B, C, D, C, B, A, B, F, C, D. You should now have 15 stripes. BO.

LEFT SIDE PANEL

Work same as right side panel, changing F to E. Note on the diagram that the left side panel is placed and sewn with row 1 at the top, reversing the stripes.

CENTER PANEL 1

First Single-Stripe Square

With B, CO 50 sts.

Row 1 (RS): P1, (K6, P6) 4 times, P1.

Row 2: K7, (P6, K6) 3 times, P6, K1.

Rows 3–60: Rep rows 1 and 2. Change to A.

First Double-Stripe Square

Row 1 (RS): With A, knit.

Row 2: Cont with A, K5, (P4, K4) 5 times, P4, K1.

Row 3: P1, (K4, P4) 6 times, P1.

Row 4: Rep row 2.

Row 5: P5, (K4, P4) 5 times, K4, P1.

Row 6: K1, (P4, K4) 6 times, K1.

Rows 7 and 8: Rep rows 5 and 6.

Row 9: P1, (K4, P4) 6 times, P1.

Rows 10–12: Rep rows 4–6.

Row 13: Purl.

Rows 14 and 15: Knit.

Rows 16 and 17: Purl.

Row 18: Knit.

Rows 19–26: Rep rows 5–12.

Rows 27–30: Rep rows 5–8. Change to D.

Rows 31–60: With D, rep rows 1–30. Change to C.

Second Single-Stripe Square

Row 1 (RS): With C, knit.

Rows 2–60: Cont with C, rep rows 2–60 of first single-stripe square. Change to A.

Second Double-Stripe Square

With A and B, work same as first double-stripe square. Change to A.

Third Single-Stripe Square

With A, work same as first single-stripe square. BO. You have now completed 2 side panels and 1 center panel.

CENTER PANEL 2

First Double-Stripe Square

With B, CO 50 sts.

Row 1: P1, (K4, P4) 6 times, P1.

Rows 2–30: Cont with B, rep rows 2–30 of first double-stripe square on center panel 1. Change to C.

Rows 31–60: With C, rep rows 31–60 of first double-stripe square on center panel 1. Change to A.

First Single-Stripe Square

Row 1 (RS): With A, knit.

Row 2: K7, (P6, K6) 3 times, P6, K1.

Row 3: P1, (K6, P6) 4 times, P1.

Row 4: K7, (P6, K6) 3 times, P6, K1.

Rows 5–60: Rep rows 1 and 2. Change to B.

Referring to diagram, cont to work as for center panel 1 in the following color sequence, always knitting the first row at each color change:

Second double-stripe square: B and A

Second single-stripe square: F

Third double-stripe square: C and D

BO.

CENTER PANEL 3

With C, CO 50 sts.

Referring to diagram, work as for center panel 1 in the following color sequence:

First single-stripe square: C

First double-stripe square: D and C

Second single-stripe square: D

Second double-stripe square: B and A

Third single-stripe square: B

CENTER PANEL 4

With B, CO 50 sts.

Referring to diagram, work as for center panel 2 in the following color sequence, with changes as noted:

First double-stripe square: B and D

Odd single-stripe square: Join E and F. Carry unused yarn loosely on WS, bringing new strand under old strand as you change colors on the following rows.

Row 1 (RS foundation row): K1 with F, (K3 with E, K3 with F) 8 times, K1 with E.

Row 2: K1 with E, (K3 with F, P3 with E) 8 times, K1 with F.

Row 3: P1 with F, (K3 with E, P3 with F) 8 times, P1 with E.

Rows 4–59: Rep rows 2 and 3.

Row 60: Rep row 2.

Second double-stripe square: A and B

Second single-stripe square: C

Third double-stripe square: D and A

LOWER AND TOP PANELS (Make 2 identical pieces)

With C, CO 32 sts.

Row 1 (RS): P1, K6, (P6, K6) twice, P1.

Row 2: K1, P6, (K6, P6) twice, K1.

Rows 3–10: Rep rows 1 and 2.

Row 11: P7, (K6, P6) twice, P1.

Row 12: K7, (P6, K6) twice, K1.

Rows 13–20: Rep rows 11 and 12.

Row 21–40: Cont with C, rep rows 1–20. Change to B.

Beg with B, work next 12 stripes as for side panel in the following color sequence: B, A, B, C, D, C, B, C, B, A, B, A. Change to C for last corner.

LAST CORNER:

Row 1: With C, knit.

Rows 2–40: Cont with C, rep rows 2–40.

BO.

ASSEMBLY

Arrange panels according to diagram. With tapestry needle and A, sew panels tog.

EDGING

Hold throw with RS facing you. With C, PU sts along one side edge, having 2 sts for every 3 rows, and 1 st in each CO and BO st, adjusting so sts lie flat. Knit 4 rows. BO on WS. Rep for other side edging. For lower and top edgings, PU 2 sts for every 3 rows, adjusting so piece lies flat. Work as for side edgings.

Assembly diagram — 50" wide by 60" tall.

C	B	A	B	C	D	C	B	C	B	A	B	A	C

Col 1	Col 2	Col 3	Col 4	Col 5	Col 6
A		D		A	D
B	A		B		C
A		C		D	F
B	B		A		B
C		F		C	A
B	A		B		B
C		A		B	C
D	C		D		D
C		B		A	C
B	D		C		B
A		A	E / F / E		C
B	A		D		B
E		C		D	A
C	B		C		B
D		B		B	A

C	A	B	A	B	C	B	C	D	C	B	A	B	C

TEA OR COFFEE?

Self-striping yarns are now available in so many textures and weights, the striping options are endless. This vest uses a brushed bulky-weight yarn knit side to side to create wide vertical stripes. The nature of the yarn, the dye method used, and the vest size will determine the width of the stripes and cause them to fall at different intervals.

Skill Level: Easy
Sizes: Small (Medium, Large)
Finished Chest: 36 (40, 44)"

MATERIALS

5 (6, 7) skeins of Merino Stripes from Crystal Palace Yarns (90% merino wool, 10% acrylic; 115 yds; 50 g), color 32 (browns) **⑤**
• Size 8 (5 mm) circular needle, 24" long, or size to obtain gauge
• Size 8 double-pointed needles (for I-cord button loop)
• Tapestry needle
• 2 buttons with shank, 1" diameter

GAUGE

18 sts and 17 rows = 4" in St st with A

Note: Vest pieces are knit from side to side.

BACK

CO 34 (34, 39) sts.

Row 1 (RS): Knit.

Row 2: Purl.

Rows 3–8: Rep rows 1 and 2.

Row 9: Knit to last 2 sts, K1f&b, K1—35 (35, 40) sts.

Row 10: Purl.

Rows 11–14: Rep rows 9 and 10 twice—37 (37, 42) sts.

Left Back Armhole and Shoulder

Row 1 (RS): Knit across; at end of needle, CO another 32 (35, 38) sts—69 (72, 80) sts.

Row 2: Purl.

Row 3: Knit.

Row 4: Purl.

Rows 5–24 (28, 32): Rep rows 3 and 4 another 10 (12, 14) times.

Next row: Rep row 3.

TRY THIS!

To match up the stripes on separate pieces as on the two front pieces, try this. Starting with an unused skein of yarn, complete one front piece. Now pick up another unused skein of yarn and pull out the strand until you reach a color section that closely matches the shade at the beginning of the finished piece. Cut the yarn at that point. (Save the cut length for sewing seams or making edgings and I-cord button loops.) Now, starting with the cut end, knit the second front piece. The color changes are subtle, so the stripes will appear to match on the left and right fronts.

   This method can also be used when a second skein of yarn is needed in the middle of a large piece, such as on the vest back. Just draw out the yarn on an unused skein until you reach the same shade as the last row knit when the yarn ran out. Cut the strand at this point and join the cut end of the skein. Always join a new skein at the beginning of a row.

Row 9: Purl.

Rows 10–15: Rep rows 8 and 9 another 3 times. BO.

RIGHT FRONT

Work same as back through left back armhole and shoulder—69 (72, 80) sts.

Right Front Neckline

Row 1 (WS): BO first 6 sts, purl across—63 (66, 74) sts.

Row 2 (RS): Knit to last 3 sts, K2tog, K1—62 (65, 73) sts.

Row 3: Purl.

Rows 4–15: Work rows 2 and 3 another 6 times—56 (59, 67) sts.

Row 16: Rep row 2—55 (58, 66) sts.

Row 17: Knit.

Row 18: Rep row 2—54 (57, 65) sts.

Row 19: Knit.

Row 20: Rep row 2—53 (56, 64) sts. BO on WS.

LEFT FRONT

CO 34 (34, 39) sts.

Row 1 (RS): Knit.

Row 2: Purl.

Rows 3–8: Rep rows 1 and 2.

Row 9: K1f&b, knit across—35 (35, 40) sts.

Row 10: Purl.

Rows 11–14: Rep rows 9 and 10 twice—37 (37, 42) sts.

Left Front Armhole and Shoulder

Row 1 (RS): CO another 32 (35, 38) sts at beg of needle, knit across—69 (72, 80) sts.

Row 2: Purl.

Row 3: Knit.

Row 4: Purl.

Rows 5–24 (28, 32): Rep rows 3 and 4 another 10 (12, 14) times.

Left Front Neckline

Row 1 (RS): BO first 6 sts, knit across—63 (66, 74) sts.

Row 2: Purl.

Row 3: K1, K2tog tbl, knit across—62 (65, 73) sts.

Left Back Neckline

Row 1 (WS): BO first 6 sts, purl across—63 (66, 74) sts.

Row 2 (RS): Knit to last 3 sts, K2tog, K1—62 (65, 73) sts.

Row 3: Purl.

Rows 4 and 5: Rep rows 2 and 3—61 (64, (72) sts. Work in St st until piece measures 12¼ (12½, 12¾)", ending on a WS row.

Right Back Neckline

Row 1 (RS): Knit to last 2 sts, K1f&b, K1—62 (65, 73) sts.

Row 2: Purl.

Rows 3 and 4: Rep rows 1 and 2—63 (66, 74) sts.

Row 5: Knit across, CO 6 sts—69 (72, 80) sts.

Row 6: Purl.

Row 7: Knit.

Rows 8–29 (33, 37): Rep rows 6 and 7 another 11 (13, 15) times.

Right Back Armhole and Shoulder

Row 1 (WS): BO first 32 (35, 38) sts, purl across—37 (37, 42) sts.

Row 2 (RS): Knit to last 3 sts, K2tog, K1—36 (36, 41) sts.

Row 3: Purl.

Rows 4–7: Rep rows 2 and 3 twice—34 (34, 39) sts.

Row 8: Knit.

Row 4: Purl.

Rows 5–16: Work rows 3 and 4 another 6 times—56 (59, 67) sts.

Row 17: Rep row 3—55 (58, 66) sts.

Row 18: Knit.

Rows 19 and 20: Rep rows 17 and 18—54 (57, 65) sts.

Row 21: Rep row 17—53 (56, 64) sts.

BO on WS.

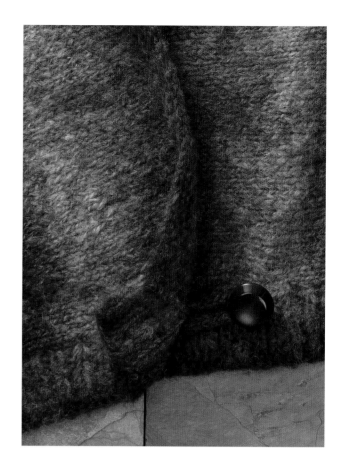

FINISHING

Sew shoulder seams.

Armhole and neck edgings: Hold vest with RS of one side edge at top. PU 2 sts for every 3 rows along armhole edge, adjusting so sts lie flat. Knit 5 rows. BO. Work other armhole and neck edgings in same manner. Sew side seams.

Lower ribbing: Hold vest with RS facing you and lower edge at top; PU 2 sts for every 3 rows in edge of each row. Work in K1, P1 ribbing for 1½ (2, 2½)". BO in ribbing.

I-cord button loop: With double-pointed needles, CO 3 sts. Do not turn.

Row 1 (RS): Slip sts to opposite end of needle, carry yarn across back, and K3. Do not turn.

Rep row 1 until button loop measures 4". BO.

Fold I-cord in half to form loop. Tack ends and sew to WS of right front placket at waist above ribbing. Sew 1 button to each front above ribbing about 3" from center edge.

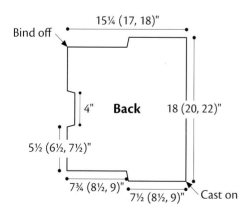

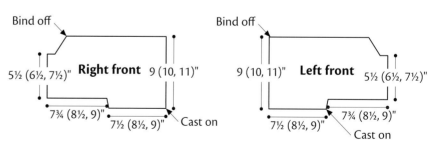

All pieces are knit sideways.

LAVENDER TEA SWEATER

The shape of this sweater works for almost any figure. The funnel collar at the neckline fits easily over most tops, and the bell-shaped cuffs add interest. The blended colors in a striated yarn are striped with matching solids.

Skill Level: Intermediate
Sizes: Small (Medium, Large)
Finished Bust: 36 (40, 44)"

MATERIALS

- **A**   9 skeins of Taos from Crystal Palace Yarns (100% wool; 128 yds; 50 g), color 1 (striated peach/blue/plum) (4)
- **B**   1 skein of Aran from Crystal Palace Yarns (100% wool; 102 yds; 50 g), color 1007 (plum) (4)
- **C**   1 skein of Aran from Crystal Palace Yarns, color 1018 (lavender)
- Size 7 (4.5 mm) circular needle, 24" long, or size to obtain gauge
- Stitch holder
- Stitch marker
- 4 safety pins
- Tapestry needle

GAUGE

20 sts and 24 rows = 4" in St st with A

SPECIAL STITCH (ON COLLAR)

M1 pw: To make 1 st on the purl side, insert RH needle from front to back under the bar between the last st and first st on LH needle, place loop on needle; insert LH needle through back of loop and P1.

Note: Carry A along side edge to reduce the number of tails to weave in. Cut B and C after each use.

BACK

With A, CO 93 (103, 113) sts.

Lower Section

Knit 6 rows for garter-st edging.

Row 7: Knit.

> ### TRY THIS!
> Leave the side seams open at the lower edges for more room at the hips. The pattern is written with garter-stitch side edges at the bottom.

Row 8: K5, purl to last 5 sts, K5.

Rows 9–18 (22, 26): Rep rows 7 and 8 another 5 (7, 9) times.

Body

Rows 1 (RS)–4: With A, knit.

Row 5: With B, knit.

Row 6: With B, purl.

Row 7: With B, K2, YO, *K2tog, YO, rep from * to last 3 sts, K2tog tbl, K1.

Row 8: With B, purl.

Rows 9–12: With A, knit.

Rows 13–24: With A, work in St st.

Rows 25–28: With A, knit.

Rows 29–32: With C, rep rows 5–8.

Rows 33–64: Rep rows 1–32 once more.

Rows 65–90: Rep rows 1–26 once.

Left Back Neckline and Shoulder

Row 1 (RS): Cont with A, K29 (33, 37), BO 35 (37, 39) sts, K29 (33, 37).

Row 2: With A, K29 (33, 37); place rem sts on st holder for right back shoulder.

Row 3: With C, K2tog, knit across—28 (32, 36) sts.

Row 4: With C, purl.

Row 5: With C, K1, *YO, K2tog, rep from * to last st, K1.

Row 6: With C, purl.

Row 7: With A, K1, K2tog, knit across—27 (31, 35) sts.

Row 8: With A, knit.

Rows 9 and 10: Rep rows 7 and 8—26 (30, 34) sts.

Rows 11–17: With A, work in St st.

BO on WS.

Right Back Neckline and Shoulder

Place 29 (33, 37) sts from holder onto needle and hold with WS facing you. Join A in first st at neckline.

Row 1 (WS): With A, knit.

Row 2 (RS): With C, knit to last 3 sts, K2tog, K1—28 (32, 36) sts.

Row 3: With C, purl.

Row 4: With C, K1, *YO, K2tog, rep from * to last st, K1.

Row 5: With C, purl.

Row 6: With A, knit to last 3 sts, K2tog, K1—27 (31, 35) sts.

Row 7: With A, knit.

Rows 8 and 9: Rep rows 6 and 7—26 (30, 34).

Rows 10–16: With A, work in St st.

BO on WS.

FRONT

Work same as back through row 78 of back body.

Right Front Neckline and Shoulder

Row 1 (RS): Cont with A, K35 (39, 43), BO 23 (25, 27) sts, K35 (39, 43).

Row 2: K35 (39, 43); place rem sts on st holder for left front shoulder.

Row 3: Cont with A, K1, K2tog, knit across—34 (38, 42) sts.

Row 4: Purl.

Rows 5–14: Work rows 3 and 4 another 5 times—29 (33, 37) sts.

Row 15: With C, K2tog, knit across—28 (32, 36) sts.

Row 16: With C, purl.

Row 17: With C, K1, *YO, K2tog, rep from * to last st, K1.

Row 18: With C, purl.

Row 19: With A, K1, K2tog, knit across—27 (31, 35) sts.

Row 20: With A, knit.

Rows 21 and 22: Rep rows 19 and 20—26 (30, 34) sts.

Rows 23–29: With A, work in St st.

BO on WS.

Left Front Neckline and Shoulder

Place 35 (39, 43) sts from holder onto needle and hold with WS facing you. Join A in first st at neckline.

Row 1 (WS): With A, knit.

Row 2 (RS): Cont with A, knit to last 3 sts, K2tog, K1—34 (38, 42) sts.

Row 3: With A, purl.

Rows 4–13: Work rows 2 and 3 another 6 times—29 (33, 37) sts.

Row 14: With C, knit to last 2 sts, K2tog—28 (32, 36) sts.

Row 15: With C, purl.

Row 16: With C, K1, *YO, K2tog, rep from * to last st, K1.

Row 17: With C, purl.

Row 18: With A, knit to last 3 sts, K2tog, K1—27 (31, 35) sts.

Row 19: With A, knit.

Rows 20 and 21: Rep rows 18 and 19—26 (30, 34) sts.

Rows 22–28: With A, work in St st.

BO on WS.

Hold front and back with RS tog and sew shoulder seams with backstitch.

SLEEVES

Mark front and back side edges 8 (8½, 9)" from shoulder seam with safety pins.

Row 1 (RS): With A and RS facing you, PU 83 (87, 91) sts between pins.

Rows 2 (WS)–12: Beg with a purl row, work in St st.

Rows 13 (RS)–16: Cont with A, knit.

Row 17: With C, knit.

Row 18: With C, purl.

Row 19: With C, K2, *YO, K2tog, rep from * to last st, K1.

Row 20: With C, purl.

Row 21: With A, K1, K2tog, knit to last 3 sts, K2tog, K1—81 (85, 89) sts.

Rows 22–24: Cont with A, knit.

Cont in stripe patt as for body, dec 1 st on each side every 6 rows 10 (10, 7) times—61 (65, 75) sts.

Cont in stripe patt, dec 1 st on each side every 4 rows 7 (9, 13) times—47 (47, 49) sts.

Cont in stripe patt without dec until sleeve measures 15 (15, 16)", ending on a purl row.

Bell Cuff

Rows 1 (RS)–4: With A, knit.

Row 5: Cont with A, K1, *K1f&b, K1, rep from * across—70 (70, 73) sts.

Row 6: Purl.

Rows 7–28: Work in St st.

Rows 29–31: Knit.

BO.

FINISHING

With tapestry needle and A, weave sleeve and side seams tog. If desired, leave side edges open about 2" at lower edge.

Collar

Note: Collar is knit in continuous rnds; mark beg of each rnd with stitch marker or thread.

Hold sweater with RS facing you; beg at left shoulder seam, PU 2 sts for every 3 rows along edges of shoulders and 1 st in each BO st across back and front.

Rnds 1–24: Purl.

Rnd 25: *P5, M1 pw, rep from * around, purl rem sts.

Rnds 26–48: Purl.

Rnd 49: Knit.

Rnd 50: Purl.

Rnd 51: Knit.

BO loosely pw. Fold collar to RS. Allow edge to roll.

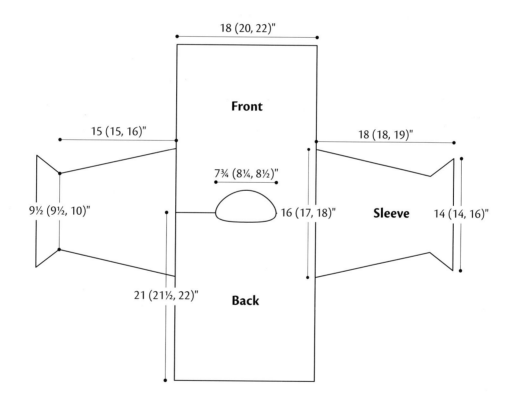

Here's the striped side.

BROWN BAG IT

Knit with a double strand of bouclé yarn throughout to obtain the look and feel of felting. No lining is required. This bag has two faces, so you can carry it with the striped side showing, or turn it around to show off the button-trimmed back.

Skill Level: Intermediate
Finished Size: 10" wide at top below handles,
12" wide at bottom, and 10" high without handles.

MATERIALS

Alpaca Boucle from Plymouth Yarn Co. (90% alpaca, 10% nylon; 65 yds; 50 g) in following amounts and colors: (5)

- **A** 4 skeins of color 11 (beige tweed)
- **B** 2 skeins of color 2 (brown tweed)
- Size 9 (5 mm) circular needle, 24" long, or size to obtain gauge
- Wood purse handles (See box below.)
- 3 decorative buttons with shanks, 1" diameter
- Yarn needle
- Sewing needle and matching thread

TRY THIS!

Bouclé yarn hides mistakes and seams well. I chose a luxurious alpaca blend for this bag because I love the feel. However, any bulky bouclé yarn will work for this trendy bag. As with most things knit, careful, detailed finishing is important, so make it a fun part of the process. Delight in watching your bag acquire shape.

CHOOSING HANDLES

Wood handles, available at most crafts and fabric stores, come in a variety of styles and widths. The top edges of the bag can be gathered to fit any handle with a slit or folded over round handles.

GAUGE

12 sts and 21 rows = 4" in St st with 2 strands of yarn held tog

Note: The bag is made in one piece, folded, and sewn at the side seams with gusseted corners on the bottom. A double strand of yarn is used throughout.

BACK TOP

With 2 strands of A held together, CO 33 sts.
Rows 1 (RS)–16: Work in rev St st, beg with a purl row.

BACK BODY

Rows 1 (RS)–24: Work in St st.
Row 25: K1f&b, knit to last 2 sts, K1f&b, K1—35 sts.
Row 26: Purl.
Row 27: Knit.
Row 28: Purl.
Rows 29–36: Rep rows 25–28 twice—39 sts.
Row 37: Knit.
Row 38: Purl.
Rows 39 and 40: Rep rows 37 and 38. Cut A.

Display the back of the purse for a different look.

BROWN BAG IT

BOTTOM

Row 1 (RS): With 2 strands of B, CO 12 sts at beg of row, knit across 39 sts—51 sts.

Row 2 (WS): CO 12 sts at beg of row, knit across 51 sts—63 sts.

Rows 3–15: Work in rev St st, beg with a purl row.

Row 16: BO first 12 sts, K39 (counting st already on RH needle), BO last 12 sts. Cut B.

FRONT BODY

Row 1 (RS): Rejoin 2 strands of A and K39.

Row 2: Purl.

Row 3: Knit.

Row 4: Purl.

Row 5: K1, K2tog tbl, knit to last 3 sts, K2tog, K1—37 sts.

Row 6: Purl.

Row 7: Knit.

Row 8: Purl. Cut A.

Rows 9–16: With B, rep rows 5–8 twice—33 sts. Cut B.

Rows 17–24: With A, rep rows 3 and 4. Cut A.

Rows 25–32: With B, rep rows 3 and 4. Cut B.

Rows 33–40: With A, rep rows 3 and 4. *Do not cut A.*

FRONT TOP

Rows 1–16: Cont with a double strand of A and beg with a purl row, work in rev St st. BO.

FINISHING

Thread yarn needle with 2 strands of B. Hold bag with WS facing you and one bottom flap at top. Fold outside flap with RS tog at open edge. Referring to the diagram below, stitch diagonally to form a gusset. Seam folded top edge of flap. Repeat for opposite side flap.

Fold one gusseted flap and sew side edges along first 16 rows of front and back. Continue to sew bag side seams, leaving top 8 rows of body and top sections open. Repeat on opposite side. Turn bag RS out.

Sew 3 buttons in a row at center of back.

Gently draw back top section halfway through slit in one handle (or place directly over round handle) and sew seam with overcast st. Rep for front handle. Weave in ends.

Note: Use the knitted cast-on to add stitches at the beginning of the row. * Insert the needle into the stitch at the beginning of the row and knit it. Place the new stitch onto the left needle as shown. Repeat from * until the desired number of stitches have been cast on. Do not turn. Begin working at the new beginning of the row.

Knit into stitch

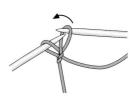

Place new stitch on left needle.

11"

3"

13"

Front

Stitch line

Bottom

Fold line

Back

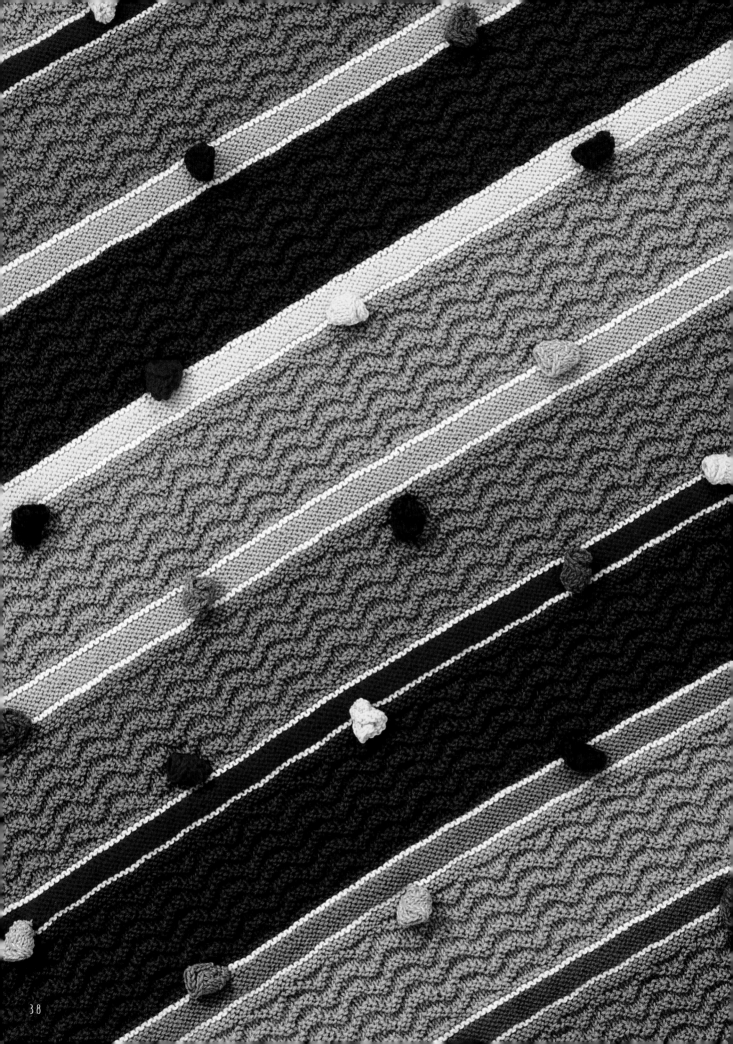

BED OF ROSES AFGHAN

Roses of many colors dance through the grass green sections of this colorful afghan. The texture and color both change in this stripe pattern, and rosebuds are knitted separately and sewn in place after the afgan is complete.

Skill Level: Easy
Size: 46" x 70"

MATERIALS

Galway from Plymouth Yarn Co. (100% wool; 210 yds; 100 g) in following amounts and colors: (4)

A	1 skein of color 8 (white)
B	4 skeins of color 130 (dark green)
C	4 skeins of color 127 (medium green)
D	4 skeins of color 121 (light green)
E	1 skein of color 117 (plum)
F	1 skein of color 89 (lavender)
G	1 skein of color 98 (light lavender)
H	1 skein of color 148 (red)

220 Superwash from Cascade Yarns (100% Superwash wool; 220 yds; 3.5 oz, 100 g) in following amounts and colors: (4)

I	1 skein of color 836 (pink)
J	1 skein of color 820 (yellow)

• Size 8 (5 mm) circular needle, at least 29" long, or size to obtain gauge

• Tapestry needle

GAUGE

18 sts and 24 rows = 4" in St st

DIRECTIONS

Note: For this project, I cut the yarn after each use. For tips on working with stripes in different yarns, see "Changing Colors and Carrying Yarns" on page 5 and decide which technique works best for you.

First Rose Patch

With B, CO 206 sts.

Rows 1 and 2: Knit.

Row 3 (RS): K6, (P2, K6) 25 times.

Row 4: K1, P4, (K4, P4) 25 times, K1.

Row 5: P2, (K2, P2) 51 times.

Row 6: P1, K4, (P4, K4) 25 times, P1.

Row 7: K2, P2, (K6, P2) 25 times, K2.

Row 8: P6, (K2, P6) 25 times.

Row 9: Rep row 6.

Row 10: K2, (P2, K2) 51 times.

Row 11: Rep row 4.

Row 12: P2, K2, (P6, K2) 25 times, P2.

Rows 13–32: Work rows 3–12 two more times.

Row 33: Purl.

Row 34: Knit.

Rows 35 and 36: With A, knit.

Rows 37 and 38: With E, knit.

Row 39: With E, purl.

Row 40: Knit.

Row 41: Purl.

Row 42: Knit.

Rows 43 and 44: With A, knit.

TRY THIS!
Place the rosebuds randomly along the colored stripes, or eliminate the rosebuds and use the leftover colors to make tassels for each corner or add fringe along the top and bottom edges.

Second Rose Patch

Work rows 1–44 in the following color sequence:

34 rows of C, 2 rows of A, 6 rows of F,
2 rows of A.

Third Rose Patch

Work rows 1–44 in the following color sequence:

34 rows of D, 2 rows of A, 6 rows of G,
2 rows of A.

Fourth Rose Patch

Work rows 1–44 in the following color sequence:

34 rows of B, 2 rows of A, 6 rows of H,
2 rows of A.

Fifth Rose Patch

Work rows 1–44 in the following color sequence:

34 rows of C, 2 rows of A, 6 rows of I,
2 rows of A.

Sixth Rose Patch

Work rows 1–44 in the following color sequence:

34 rows of D, 2 rows of A, 6 rows of J,
2 rows of A.

Seventh Rose Patch

Work rows 1–44 in the following color sequence:

34 rows of B, 2 rows of A, 6 rows of I,
2 rows of A.

Eighth Rose Patch

Work rows 1–44 in the following color sequence:

34 rows of C, 2 rows of A, 6 rows of H,
2 rows of A.

Ninth Rose Patch

Work rows 1–44 in the following color sequence:

34 rows of D, 2 rows of A, 6 rows of G,
2 rows of A.

Tenth Rose Patch

Work rows 1–44 in the following color sequence:

34 rows of B, 2 rows of A, 6 rows of F,
2 rows of A.

Eleventh Rose Patch

Work rows 1–44 in the following color sequence:

34 rows of C, 2 rows of A, 6 rows of E,
2 rows of A.

With D, work rows 1–33.

BO.

Rosebuds (Make 11 each in E, F, G, H, I, and J)

CO 5 sts, leaving an 8" tail for sewing.

Row 1 (RS): Knit.

Row 2: K1f&B in first 4 sts, K1—9 sts.

Row 3: Knit.

Row 4: K1f&b in first 8 sts, K1—17 sts.

Row 5: Knit.

Row 6: Purl.

Row 7: Knit.

BO.

Beg at row 1, roll each rosebud into shape. Thread tails into tapestry needle and, referring to photo, tack rosebuds randomly on each rose-colored stripe. Weave in ends.

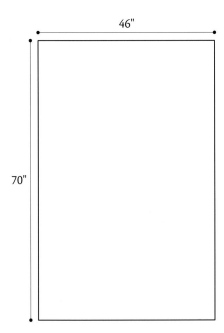

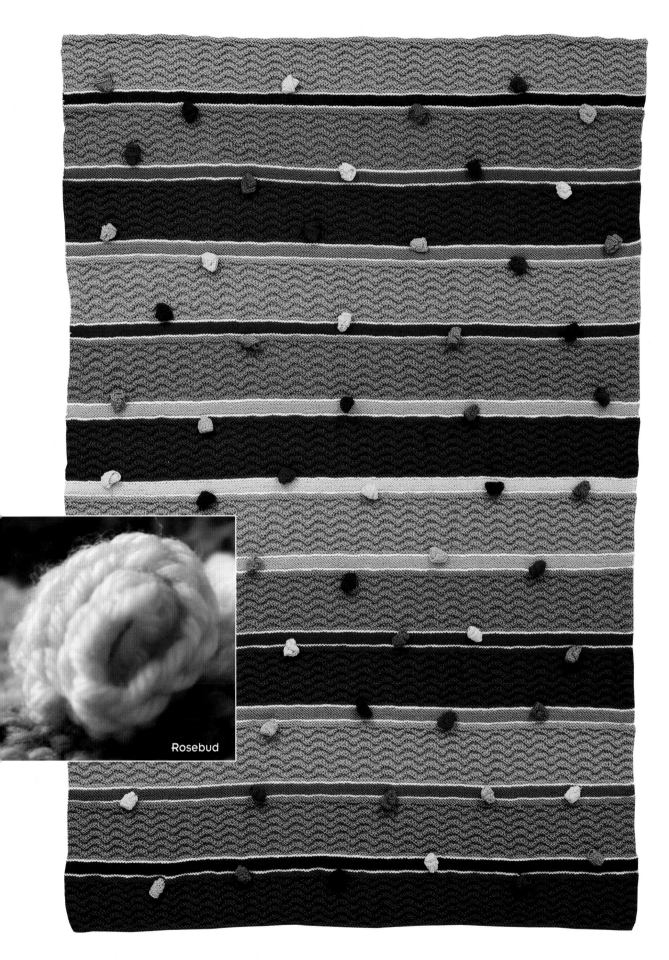

Rosebud

SHAWL-COLLAR JACKET

How fulfilling to knit yourself a warm, oversized, easily constructed jacket to slip on when the weather changes. Knit with a yummy striated yarn and matching solids, the jacket has a shawl collar with the same rib pattern as the lower body and sleeves. There is a lot of yarn in this jacket, and the initial investment may be high, but this is one time you may want to splurge a little.

Skill Level: Intermediate
Sizes: Small (Medium, Large)
Finished Bust: 42 (45, 48)"

MATERIALS

- A   10 (12, 14) skeins of Cleckheaton Country 8 ply from Plymouth Yarn Co. (100% new wool; 105 yds, 95 m; 50 g), color 48 (navy) (3)
- B   3 (3, 4) skeins of Country 8 ply, color 2265 (green)
- C   4 (4, 4) skeins of Taos from Crystal Palace Yarns (100% wool; 128 yds, 118 m; 50 g), color 10 (striated blue/red/brown) (3)

- Size 8 (5 mm) circular needle, at least 32" long, or size to obtain gauge (length is necessary for collar)
- 2 size 8 (5 mm) double-pointed needles (for I-cord button loop)
- Tapestry needle
- 4 safety pins
- 1 decorative button with shank, 1" diameter

> **TRY THIS!**
> Use a quality wool that is easy to care for and will afford you many years of comfortable wear.

GAUGE

18 sts and 24 rows = 4" in St st with A

BACK

Note: For this project, I cut the yarn after each use. For tips on working with stripes in different yarns, see "Changing Colors and Carrying Yarns" on page 5 and decide which technique works best for you.

Ribbing Section

With A, CO 125 (137, 145) sts.

Row 1 (RS): With A, P1, *K3, P1, rep from * across.

Row 2: With A, K2, P1, *K3, P1, rep from * to last 2 sts, K2.

Rows 3–10: With A, rep rows 1 and 2 another 4 times.

Rows 11–14: With B, rep rows 1 and 2 twice.

Rows 15–24: With A, rep rows 1 and 2 another 5 times.

Rows 25–34: With C, rep rows 1 and 2 another 5 times.

Rows 35–38: With B, rep rows 1 and 2 twice.

Rows 39–48: With C, rep rows 1 and 2 another 5 times.

Rows 49–96: Rep rows 1–48.

Top Section

SMALL SIZE ONLY:

Row 1 (RS): With A, P1, (K3, P1) twice; *K2tog, K1, P1, rep from * to last 8 sts, (K3, P1) twice—98 sts.

MEDIUM AND LARGE SIZES ONLY:

Row 1 (RS): With A, P1, *K2tog, K1, P1, rep from * across—103 (109) sts.

Row 2: With A, purl.

Row 3: With A, knit.

Row 4: With A, purl.

Rows 5–10: With A, rep rows 3 and 4 another 3 times.

Rows 11–14: With B, rep rows 3 and 4 twice.

Rows 15–24: With A, rep rows 3 and 4 another 5 times.

Rows 25–34: With C, rep rows 3 and 4 another 5 times.

Rows 35–38: With B, rep rows 3 and 4 twice.

Rows 39–48: With C, rep rows 3 and 4 another 5 times.

Row 49: With A, rep row 3.

Rows 50–72: Rep rows 2–24.

BO.

LEFT FRONT

With A, CO 57 (65, 73) sts.

Rows 1–96: Rep rows 1–96 of back ribbing section.

Top Section

SMALL SIZE ONLY:

Row 1 (RS): With A, P1, (K3, P1) twice; *K2tog, K1, P1, rep from * across—45 sts.

MEDIUM AND LARGE SIZES ONLY:

Row 1 (RS): With A, P1, *K2tog, P1, rep from * across—49 (55) sts.

ALL SIZES:

Row 2: With A, purl.

Row 3: With A, knit to last 3 sts, K2tog, K1—44 (48, 54) sts.

Row 4: With A, purl.

Rows 5–72: Cont in stripe patt as for back, dec 1 st as in row 3 every 2 rows 0 (4, 6) more times and every 4 rows 17 (15, 14) times—27 (29, 34) sts.

BO.

RIGHT FRONT

With A, CO 57 (65, 73) sts.

Rows 1–96: Rep rows 1–96 of back ribbing section.

Top Section

SMALL SIZE ONLY:

Row 1 (RS): With A, P1, *K2tog, K1, P1, rep from * to last 8 sts, (K3, P1) twice—45 sts.

MEDIUM AND LARGE SIZES ONLY:

Row 1 (RS): With A, P1, *K2tog, P1, rep from * across—49 (55) sts.

ALL SIZES:

Row 2: With A, purl.

Row 3: With A, K1, K2tog tbl, knit across—44 (48, 54) sts.

Row 4: With A, purl.

Rows 5–72: Cont in stripe patt as for back, dec 1 st as in row 3 every 2 rows 0 (4, 6) more times and every 4 rows 17 (15, 14) times—27 (29, 34) sts.

BO. Sew shoulder seams.

SLEEVES (Make 2)

With A, CO 81 sts (all sizes).

Rows 1–48: Rep rows 1–48 of back ribbing section.

Row 49: With A, knit.

Row 50: With A, purl.

Row 51: With A, K1f&b, knit to last 2 sts, K1f&b, K1—83 sts.

Row 52: With A, purl.

Rows 53–120: Cont in stripe patt and St st, inc as in row 51 every 6 rows 4 (4, 6) more times—91 (91, 95) sts.

Sleeve Cap

Row 1 (RS): K1, K2tog tbl, knit to last 3 sts, K2tog, K1—89 (89, 93) sts.

Row 2: Purl.

Rows 3–10: Rep rows 1 and 2 another 4 times—81 (81, 85) sts.

BO.

SHAWL COLLAR

Hold right front with RS facing you. With A, PU 1 st in edge of each row along right center front, in each BO st across back, and in edge of each row along left center front, adjusting to a multiple of 4+1 (see "Picking Up Stitches" box on page 47 for tips).

Row 1 (WS): K2, P1, *K3, P1, rep from * to last 2 sts, K2.

Row 2 (RS): P1, *K3, P1, rep from * across.

Row 3: K2, P1, *K3, P1, rep from * to last 2 sts, K2.

Begin short rows:

Note: The exact stitch location of the turn is not important. Just be sure to stay in pattern as you work the short rows.

PICKING UP STITCHES

It can be frustrating to pick up a large number of stitches only to discover you do not have the correct number required for your pattern. Here's an easy fix: Slide all stitches to the opposite end of your circular needle and pull out the last 20 to 30 stitches (the first 20 to 30 stitches picked up). Now pick up the stitches necessary to arrive at the correct number. A missed row or two will not be a problem. You can use a crochet hook to pick up the stitches.

Row 4: P1, *K3, P1, rep around to top of rib section on left front, *K1, yf, sl 1, yb, turn, slip st back to RH needle*, work in patt to top of ribbing on right front, rep from * to * once more, work in patt across.

Row 5: Rep row 3.

Row 6: P1, *K3, P1, rep around to B stripe above ribbing on left front, *K1, yf, sl 1, yb, turn, slip st back to RH needle*, work in patt to B stripe above ribbing on right front, rep from * to * once more, work in patt across.

Row 7: Rep row 3.

Row 8: P1, *K3, P1, rep around to top of A stripe above ribbing on left front, *K1, yf, sl 1, yb, turn, slip st back to RH needle*, work in patt to top of A stripe above ribbing on right front, rep from * to * once more, work in patt across.

Row 9: Rep row 3.

Row 10: P1, *K3, P1, rep around to second B stripe on left front, K1, yf, sl 1, yb, turn, slip st back to RH needle*, work in patt to second B stripe on right front, rep from * to * once more, work in patt across.

Note: You have added 8 rows to the collar at the top front sections and across the back.

Row 11: Rep row 3.

Rows 12–17: Rep rows 2 and 3 another 3 times.

You should now have 17 rows (including PU row) along ribbing on both fronts and 25 rows at center back. BO in rib patt.

I-CORD BUTTON LOOP

With double-pointed needles and A, CO 3 sts.

Row 1: Slip sts to opposite end of needle; bring yarn behind sts to beg of needle and K3.

Rep row 1 until I-cord measures about 2". BO.

The jacket can be worn open or buttoned.

FINISHING

Mark front and back sections 9 (9, 9½)" below shoulder seams. With RS tog, tapestry needle, and A, sew sleeves to body between marks from beg to end of sleeve caps, easing to fit. Sew underarm and side seams. Sew button to center left front ribbing about 2" above body ribbing. Fold I-cord in half to form a loop and tack ends opposite button on WS of right front.

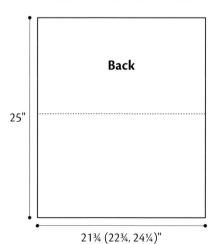

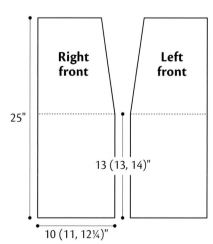

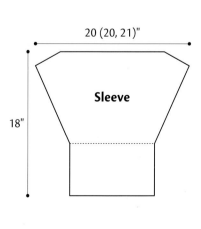

Back — 25" — 21¾ (22¾, 24¼)"

Right front / **Left front** — 25" — 13 (13, 14)" — 10 (11, 12¼)"

Sleeve — 20 (20, 21)" — 18"

SPRING RIBBONS AFGHAN

Narrow stripes in jewel tones set in an off-white background suggest a party atmosphere. This afghan is easy to knit and suitable for most beginners.

Skill Level: Easy
Size: 45" x 64"

MATERIALS

220 Superwash from Cascade Yarns (100% Superwash wool; 220 yds, 3.5 oz; 100 g) in following amounts and colors: (4)

MC	7 skeins of color 817 (off-white)
A	1 skein of color 836 (pink)
B	1 skein of color 804 (amethyst)
C	1 skein of color 851 (light emerald)
D	1 skein of color 876 (topaz)
E	1 skein of color 807 (ruby)
F	1 skein of color 842 (lilac)
G	1 skein of color 802 (emerald)
H	1 skein of color 843 (violet)

- Size 8 (5 mm) circular needle, 29" long, or size to obtain gauge
- Size H-8 (5 mm) crochet hook for attaching fringe
- Tapestry needle

GAUGE

18 sts and 24 rows = 4" in St st

DIRECTIONS

Note: For this project, I carried A along the side edges and cut the other colors after each use. For tips on working with stripes in different yarns, see "Changing Colors and Carrying Yarns" on page 5 and decide which technique works best for you.

Note: When slipping stitches in this pattern, the yarn should always be held on the wrong side of the work. Because the right side of the ribbons are purled, you must move the yarn to the back when slipping stitches on right-side rows. On wrong-side rows, bring the yarn to the front before slipping stitches. All stitches are slipped purlwise.

With MC, CO 206 sts.

Rows 1–3 (RS): With MC, knit.

Row 4: With MC, purl.

Row 5: With A, K6, sl 2 pw wyib, (K14, sl 2 pw wyib) 12 times, K6.

Row 6: With A, K6, sl 2 pw wyif, (K14, sl 2 pw wyif) 12 times, K6.

Row 7: With A, P6, sl 2 pw wyib, (P14, sl 2 pw wyib) 12 times, P6.

Row 8: Rep row 6.

Row 9: With MC, knit.

Row 10: With MC, purl.

Row 11: With MC, knit.

Row 12: With B, P14, sl 2 pw wyif, (P14, sl 2 pw wyif) 11 times, P14.

Row 13: With B, P14, sl 2 pw wyib, (P14, sl 2 pw wyib) 11 times, P14.

TRY THIS!

Since each color requires only one 3 ounce (100 g) skein of worsted-weight yarn, this afghan is a great way to use up leftover yarn. Gather eight colors, add seven skeins of the main color, and knit an afghan that is uniquely yours. Try using black or navy blue as the main color. Or, alternate only two dark colors against a light main-color background.

Row 14: With B, K14, sl 2 pw wyif, (K14, sl 2 pw wyif) 11 times, K14.

Row 15: With B, rep row 13.

Row 16: With MC, purl.

Row 17: With MC, knit.

Row 18: With MC, purl.

Rep rows 5–18 another 7 times in the following color sequence:

C	4 rows
MC	3 rows
D	4 rows
MC	3 rows
E	4 rows
MC	3 rows
F	4 rows
MC	3 rows
G	4 rows
MC	3 rows
H	4 rows
*MC	3 rows
A	4 rows
MC	3 rows
B	4 rows
MC	3 rows
C	4 rows
MC	3 rows
D	4 rows
MC	3 rows
E	4 rows
MC	3 rows
F	4 rows
MC	3 rows
G	4 rows
MC	3 rows
H	4 rows*

Rep color sequence from * to * until afghan measures about 63", ending with 4 rows of H.

With MC, purl 2 rows, then knit 1 row. BO all sts.

FRINGE

Cut 412 strands of MC 16" long. Use the crochet hook to attach a single strand of fringe to each CO and BO st. Trim ends even.

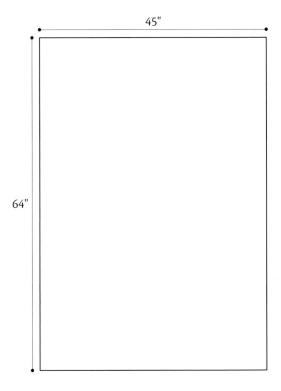

SPRING RIBBONS AFGHAN

SPRING RIBBONS AFGHAN

DESERT HEAT AFGHAN

Choose hot reds and lavenders, then mix them with shades of desert golds and rusts. Arrange them in graduated steps of glorious color leading to the hot red center. Add tassels as shown in the photos, or place them at the bottom and top corners for a more traditional look. This afghan, worked in four sections, is easy to knit, but care is needed in assembly.

Skill Level: Intermediate

Size: Approx 52" x 64"

Note: This afghan may stretch and the final measurements may vary slightly.

MATERIALS

220 Superwash from Cascade Yarns (100% Superwash wool; 220 yds, 3.5 oz; 100 g) in following amounts and colors: (**4**)

- A   3 skeins of color 843 (fuchsia)
- B   3 skeins of color 807 (dark rose)
- C   2 skeins of color 804 (lavender)
- D   2 skeins of color 837 (rose)
- E   1 skein of color 808 (red)
- F   3 skeins of color 876 (gold)
- G   3 skeins of color 822 (dark orange)
- H   2 skeins of color 823 (rust)

- Size 8 (5 mm) circular needle, at least 29" long, or size to obtain gauge
- Tapestry needle
- Crochet hook (for tassels)

GAUGE

Approx 16 sts and 32 rows = 4" in pattern stitch

To work a gauge swatch, first see "Special Abbreviation" at right. With A, CO 17 sts.

Knit 2 foundation rows, then begin patt:

Row 1: With B, K1, (K1b, K1) 20 times.

Row 2: With B, knit.

Row 3: With A, K2, (K1b, K1) 18 times, K2.

Row 4: With A, knit.

Rows 5–32: Rep rows 1–4.

BO. Your swatch should measure 4" x 4¼" with foundation rows.

> **TRY THIS!**
> Substitute a pastel color palette of lavenders, pinks, and yellows to create the look of a romantic sunset on a Caribbean beach.

SPECIAL ABBREVIATION

K1b: Knit 1 in corresponding stitch in second row below.

TOP AND BOTTOM SECTIONS
(Make 2 identical pieces)

The sections are knitted from the top and bottom edges toward the center. The ends meet at the center of the afghan.

Note: For this project, I carried the unused yarn along the side edge within each stripe. For tips on working with stripes in different yarns, see "Changing Colors and Carrying Yarns" on page 5 and decide which technique works best for you.

First Stripe

With A, CO 209 sts.

Rows 1 and 2: Knit.

Row 3 (RS): With B, K1, *K1b, K1; rep from * across.

Row 4: With B, knit.

Row 5: With A, K2, *K1b, K1; rep from * to last st, K1.

Row 6: With A, knit.

Rows 7–50: Rep rows 2–6 another 11 times.

Second Stripe

Row 1 (RS): With B, BO first 25 sts, knit across—184 sts.

Row 2: With B, BO first 25 sts pw, knit across—159 sts.

Rows 3 and 4: With B, knit.

Row 5: With C, K2, *K1b, K1, rep from * to last st, K1.

Row 6: With C, knit.

Row 7: With B, K1, *K1b, K1, rep from * across.

Row 8: With B, knit.

Rows 9–52: Rep rows 5–8 another 11 times.

Third Stripe

Row 1 (RS): With C, BO first 25 sts, knit across—134 sts.

Row 2: With C, BO first 25 sts pw, knit across—109 sts.

Rows 3 and 4: With C, knit.

Row 5: With D, K1, *K1b, K1, rep from * across.

Row 6: With D, knit.

Row 7: With C, K2, *K1b, K1, rep from * to last st, K1.

Row 8: With C, knit.

Rows 9–52: Rep rows 5–8 another 11 times.

Fourth Stripe

Row 1 (RS): With D, BO first 25 sts, knit across—84 sts.

Row 2: With D, BO first 25 sts pw, knit across—59 sts.

Rows 3 and 4: With D, knit.

Row 5: With E, K2, *K1b, K1, rep from * to last st, K1.

Row 6: With E, knit.

Row 7: With D, K1, *K1b, K1, rep from * across.

Row 8: With D, knit.

Rows 9–52: Rep rows 5–8 another 11 times.

Fifth Stripe

Rows 1 (RS)–4: With E, knit—59 sts.

Row 5: With H, K2, *K1b, K1, rep from * to last st, K1.

Row 6: With H, knit.

Row 7: With E, K1, *K1b, K1, rep from * across.

Row 8: With E, knit.

Rows 9–52: Rep rows 5–8 another 11 times. BO.

SIDE SECTIONS (Make 2 identical pieces)

The side sections are knitted from the outside edge toward the center. They fit into the empty spaces between the two end sections.

Sixth Stripe

With F, CO 209 sts.

Rows 1 and 2: Knit.

Row 3 (RS): With A, K1, *K1b, K1; rep from * across.

Row 4: With A, knit.

Row 5: With F, K2, *K1b, K1; rep from * to last st, K1.

Row 6: With F, knit.

Rows 7–50: Rep rows 3–6 another 11 times.

Seventh Stripe

Row 1 (RS): With G, BO first 25 sts, knit across—184 sts.

Row 2: With G, BO first 25 sts pw, knit across—159 sts.

Rows 3 and 4: With G, knit.

Row 5: With F, K2, *K1b, K1, rep from * to last st, K1.

Row 6: With F, knit.

Row 7: With G, K1, *K1b, K1, rep from * across.

Row 8: With G, knit.

Rows 9–52: Rep rows 5–8 another 11 times.

Eighth Stripe

Row 1 (RS): With H, BO first 25 sts, knit across—134 sts.

Row 2: With H, BO first 25 sts pw, knit across—109 sts.

Rows 3 and 4: With H, knit.

Row 5: With G, K1, *K1b, K1, rep from * across.

Row 6: With G, knit.

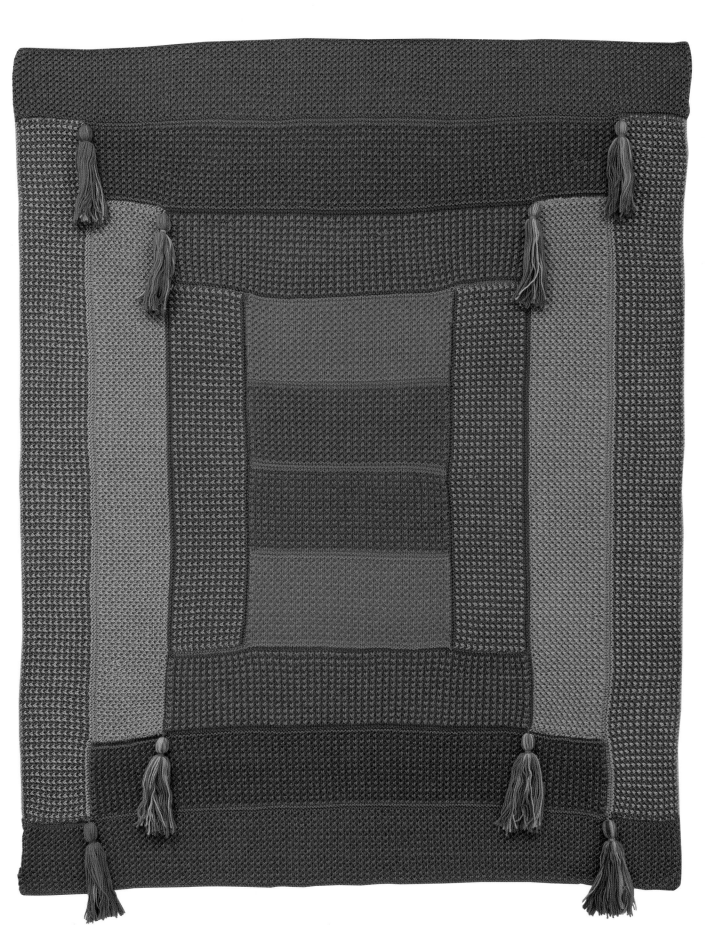

Row 7: With H, K2, *K1b, K1, rep from * to last st, K1.

Row 8: With H, knit.

Rows 9–52: Rep rows 5–8 another 11 times. BO.

ASSEMBLY

Referring to the diagram on page 59, sew sections together, easing to fit. If necessary, lightly steam assembled afghan on wrong side. Do not touch iron to afghan.

TASSELS (Make 8)

Cut 42 strands of each color 18" in length. Divide into 8 groups of 5 strands each per color. Lay 1 group of 40 strands flat and tie at the center with an extra strand of any color. Pick up by the tie ends and shake to mix colors and form a tassel of 80 strands. Wrap an extra strand of any color tightly around all 80 strands about 1" below the center tie. Using a crochet hook, hide ends. Referring to photo and using tie ends, attach 1 tassel at each lower corner of stripes 3 and 2. Alternately, attach 2 tassels to each afghan corner.

Weave in ends.

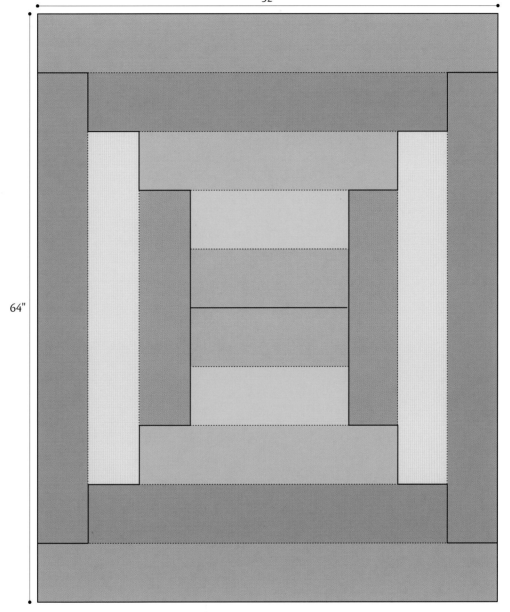

CHILI PEPPERS HAT AND SCARF

Hot and spicy colors define this very easy scarf and hat. Knit lengthwise, the scarf can be finished in a couple of hours. Both cap and scarf can be made in one evening.

A great project for using leftover skeins of yarn, almost any three colors will work for this super-easy wardrobe accent. Here's your rainy-evening gift-making project. Just keep your bind-off tension the same as your cast-on tension, and go for it!

Skill Level: Easy
Hat Size: Fits 20"–22" head
Scarf Size: Approx 2¾" x 56"

MATERIALS

Fjord from Crystal Palace Yarns (100% wool; 91 yds, 84 m; 1.75 oz, 50 g) in the following amounts and colors: (4)

A	2 skeins of color 4674 Lacquer Red
B	1 skein of color 4105 Mandarin Orange
C	1 skein of color 4891 Strawberry Pink

Note: Two skeins of A and 1 skein each of B and C will make both projects.

• **Hat:** Size 8 (5 mm) needles or size to obtain gauge

• **Scarf:** Size 8 (5 mm) circular needle, 32" or longer, or size to obtain gauge

• Tapestry needle

> **TRY THIS!**
> Make the set in a self-striping yarn instead, or use shades of brown with orange autumn leaves.

GAUGE

16 sts and 24 rows = 4" in St st

Note: Row gauge is not critical for scarf.

HAT

This hat is knitted back and forth, and a back seam is sewn after the knitting is complete.

Note: For this project, I explain when I cut each yarn within the instructions. For tips on working with stripes in different yarns, see "Changing Colors and Carrying Yarns" on page 5 and decide which technique works best for you.

Ribbing

With A, CO 85 sts.

Row 1 (RS): K1, *P1, K1, rep from * across.

Row 2: P1, *K1, P1, rep from * across.

Rows 3–10: Work rows 1 and 2 another 4 times.

Body

Rows 1 (RS)–5: With A, knit.

Row 6: With A, purl.

Row 7: With A, knit.

Row 8: With A, purl. Cut A, leaving an 8" tail for sewing.

Row 9: With B, knit.

Row 10: With B, purl.

Row 11: With B, K2, *YO, K2tog, rep from * to last st, K1.

Row 12: With B, purl. Cut B, leaving an 8" tail for sewing.

Rows 13–15: With C, knit.

Row 16: With C, purl.

Rows 17–20: With C, knit. Cut C, leaving an 8" tail for sewing.

Rows 21–40: Rep rows 1–20 once more.

Crown

Row 1 (RS): With A, K3, (K2tog, K5) 11 times, K2tog, K3—73 sts.

Row 2: Purl.

Row 3: K2, (K2tog, K4) 11 times, K2tog, K3—61 sts.

Row 4: Purl.

Row 5: K1, (K2tog, K3) 12 times—49 sts.

Row 6: Purl.

Row 7: (K2tog, K2) 12 times, K1—37 sts.

Row 8: Purl.

Row 9: (K2tog, K1) 12 times, K1—25 sts.

Row 10: Purl.

Row 11: K2tog 12 times, K1—13 sts.

Row 12: Knit. Cut, leaving a 12" tail for sewing.

Thread tail into tapestry needle and, beg with last st, weave through rem sts on needle. Remove needle and draw up tight. Carefully matching colored tails and rows, weave back seam. Weave in ends.

Chili Peppers (Make 1 with A and 1 with C)

Leaving a 6" tail, CO 3 sts.

Row 1 (RS): K1f&b twice, K1—5 sts.

Row 2: Purl.

Row 3: K1, K1f&b twice, K2—7 sts.

Row 4: Purl.

Row 5: K2, K1f&b twice, K3—9 sts.

Row 6: Purl.

Row 7: K3, K1f&b twice, K4—11 sts.

Row 8: Purl.

Row 9: Knit.

Row 10: Purl.

Row 11: K4, sl 1 kw, K2tog, psso, K4—9 sts.

Row 12: Purl.

Row 13: K3, sl 1 kw, K2tog, psso, K3—7 sts.

Row 14: Purl.

Row 15: Sl 1 kw, K1, psso, sl 1 kw, K2tog, psso, K2tog—3 sts.

Row 16: Purl.

Row 17: Sl 1 kw, K2tog, psso. Draw loop on needle up about 6"; cut yarn.

Referring to photo for placement, tack peppers to hat. Weave in ends.

SCARF

SUBSTITUTING YARNS FOR THE SCARF
Use any three yarns of equal weight for this scarf and an appropriately sized needle. The width and length may change, but the scarf will be beautiful. When casting on, proper tension is usually obtained when stitches slide back and forth easily on the needle.

Note: For this project, I explain when I cut each yarn with the instructions. For tips on working with stripes in different yarns, see "Changing Colors and Carrying Yarns" on page 5 and decide which technique works best for you.

With A, loosely CO 224 sts.

Rows 1 (RS)–3: With A, knit.

Row 4: With A, purl.

Rows 5 and 6: With A, knit. Cut A.

Row 7: With B, knit.

Row 8: With B, purl.

Row 9: With B, K2, *YO, K2tog, rep from * across.

Row 10: With B, purl. Cut B.

Rows 11–13: With C, knit.

Row 14: With C, purl.

Rows 15–17: With C, knit.

BO loosely. Weave in ends.

Chili Peppers

Following directions on page 62, make 4 peppers: 2 with A, 1 with B, and 1 with C. With tapestry needle and tails and referring to photo for placement, securely tack 1 red and 1 pink pepper to one end of scarf. Tack 1 red and 1 orange pepper to opposite end.

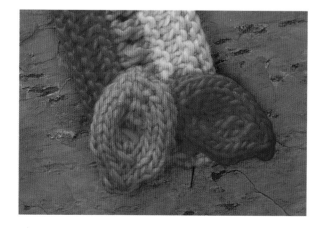

HOT STRIPES BAG

Dream about your next vacation as you knit this hot summer bag. Knit side to side and using short rows for shaping, this is a great weekend project!

Never knit in short rows? This is a simple project on which to learn. The details are clearly spelled out in the pattern, and the bulky yarn lets you see how the shaping occurs.

Skill Level: Easy/Intermediate (short rows)
Size: 16" wide at bottom x 10" high

MATERIALS

Iceland from Crystal Palace Yarns (100% wool; 109 yds, 100 m; 3.5 oz, 100 g) in following amounts and colors: (**5**)

- A   1 skein of color 8166 Sienna
- B   1 skein of color 4892 Brandy
- C   1 skein of color 4043 Forest
- D   1 skein of color 1208 Pale Sea Green

- Size 9 (5.5 mm) circular needle, 29" long, or size to obtain gauge
- Tapestry needle
- 9"-diameter or larger round purse handles (available at most crafts and fabric stores)
- 2 purchased tassels (optional)

GAUGE

16 sts and 26 rows = 4" in garter stitch (knit every row)

DIRECTIONS

Bag is worked side to side.

Note: For this project, I cut the yarn after each use. For tips on working with stripes in different yarns, see "Changing Colors and Carrying Yarns" on page 5 and decide which technique works best for you.

Beg at one side edge with A, CO 84 sts.

Rows 1 (RS) and 2: With A, knit.

Row 3 (short row): With A, K72, *yf, slip next st to RH needle, yb, turn; slip st back to needle (now on your right), yb, *K60, rep from * to * once more; knit across. You have now added 1 row over 12 sts at each end and added 2 additional rows over the center 60 sts.

Row 4: With A, knit.

Rows 5 and 6: Rep rows 3 and 4.

> ## TRY THIS!
> For a different look, change to a neutral color palette for fall, or pastels for spring. If you can't find the large, round handles used on the model, purchase a metal ring and cover it with single crochet in one of the bag colors. A thick, soft cotton rope works well also. Just tie the ends to form a circle. Let the ends show at one side of the bag. The big knot will become part of the detail and add interest to the bag.

> ## KEEPING TRACK OF SHORT ROWS
> Count the ridges. Do not count the cast-on row. You should have 3 ridges (6 rows) at each end and 5 ridges (10 rows) along the center. Four rows have been added to the width of the bag.

Row 7: With B, knit.

Row 8: With B, purl.

Rows 9 and 10: With B, rep rows 7 and 8.

Rows 11 and 12: With C, knit.

Rows 13–16: With B, rep rows 7 and 8 twice.

Rows 17 and 18: With D, knit.

Rows 19 (short row) and 20: With D, rep rows 3 and 4.

Row 21: With C, knit.

Row 22: With C, purl.

Rows 23 and 24: With D, knit.

Rows 25 and 26: With D, rep rows 3 and 4.

Rows 27–36: Beg with B, rep rows 7–16.

Rows 37–42: With A, rep rows 1–6.

Rows 43–72: Beg with B, rep rows 7–36.

Rows 73–76: With A, rep rows 3–6.

Rows 77 and 78: With A, knit.

BO.

FINISHING

Hold piece with WS facing you and one short end at top. Fold end over one handle. With tapestry needle and A, sew on WS with overcast st. Attach other handle in same manner. Fold in half with WS facing you. With tapestry needle and A, sew side seams with overcast st, leaving 3" open on each side at top. Turn bag RS out. If desired, attach one tassel at top of each side seam. Weave in ends.

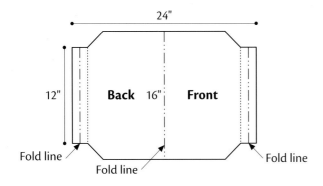

SOFT AND SWEET

Matched set of four pillows—plus one in an alternate color combination

The pillows are pretty on the back side, too.

SUNSHINE PILLOWS

Yellow can brighten any corner of your home. It's the one color guaranteed to suggest warmth and to cause the viewer to smile. Shades of yellow vary from hot gold to baby yellow, with each shade able to set a mood in your room or on your porch. Choose the color of cornmeal, then add white and cornflower blue to make this charming set.

Skill Level: Easy
Size: 14" square

MATERIALS

Galway from Plymouth Yarn Co. (100% wool; 210 yds; 100 g) (4)

Note: Each pillow requires 2 skeins of backing color and 1 skein each of 2 additional colors. All 5 pillows can be made with 3 skeins of color A, 2 skeins each of colors B, C, and D, and 1 skein of color E.

Mellow Yellow Pillow

A	2 skeins of color 104 (cornmeal)
B	1 skein of color 83 (cornflower blue)
C	1 skein of color 8 (white)

Cornflower Pillow

B	2 skeins of color 83 (cornflower blue)
A	1 skein of color 104 (cornmeal)
C	1 skein of color 8 (white)

White Sands Pillow

A	2 skeins of color 104 (cornmeal)
C	1 skein of color 8 (white)
B	1 skein of color 83 (cornflower blue)

Sail-Away Pillow

C	2 skeins of color 8 (white)
B	1 skein of color 83 (cornflower blue)
A	1 skein of color 104 (cornmeal)

Oceans Pillow

D	2 skeins of color 121 (light green)
E	1 skein of color 15 (navy)
A	1 skein of color 8 (white)

All Pillows

- Size 8 (5 mm) needles or size to obtain gauge
- 14" pillow forms (1 for each pillow)
- Tapestry needle

TRY THIS!

Substitute the cornflower blue and white with one of these combinations, always keeping the yellow: Change the cornflower blue to pastel green and substitute melon for white. Or change the cornflower blue to denim or navy as in "Oceans Pillow" shown on page 71. When making a set of pillows, use only one color for each back. This allows you to group the pillows in a variety of ways.

GAUGE

20 sts and 24 rows = 4" in St st

Note: Both stitch and row gauges are important for the pillow covering to fit snugly on the pillow form.

NOT ALL PILLOW FORMS ARE CREATED EQUAL

Take your measuring tape with you when shopping at your crafts or fabric store, and look for forms that are firmly stuffed at the corners. If you are unable to purchase good forms, buy the best you can find and stuff the corners yourself. Carefully open one seam just a few inches and stuff the corners with batting or yarn scraps. Sew the seam closed by hand with an overcast stitch or by machine.

MELLOW YELLOW PILLOW

All of the pillows are made the same way with different color sequences for the stripes.

Note: For this project, I cut the yarn after each use. For tips on working with stripes in different yarns, see "Changing Colors and Carrying Yarns" on page 5 and decide which technique works best for you.

Front

With A, CO 72 sts.

Row 1 (RS): With A, P5, *(K1 tbl, P1) 3 times, K1 tbl, P4, rep from * another 5 times, P1.

Row 2: With A, K5, *(P1, K1 tbl) 3 times, P1, K4, rep from * another 5 times, K1.

Rows 3–12: Rep rows 1 and 2 another 5 times.

Row 13: With B, K5, *(K1 tbl, K1) 3 times, K1 tbl, K4, rep from * another 5 times, K1.

Row 14: With B, rep row 2.

Rows 15 and 16: With B, rep rows 1 and 2.

Row 17: With C, rep row 13.

Row 18: With C, rep row 2.

Row 19: With B, rep row 13.

Row 20: With B, rep row 2.

Rows 21 and 22: With B, rep rows 1 and 2 once.

Row 23: With A, rep row 13.

Row 24: With A, rep row 2.

Rows 25–30: With A, rep rows 1 and 2 another 3 times.

Row 31: With C, rep row 13.

Row 32: With C, rep row 2.

Row 33: With B, rep row 13.

Row 34: With B, rep row 2.

Rows 35–44: With B, rep rows 1 and 2 another 5 times.

Row 45: With C, rep row 13.

Row 46: With C, rep row 2.

You have now completed the center stripe of the pillow front.

Row 47: With B, rep row 13.

Row 48: With B, rep row 2.

Rows 49–58: With B, rep rows 1 and 2 another 5 times.

Row 59: With C, rep row 13.

Row 60: With C, rep row 2.

Row 61: With A, rep row 13.

Row 62: With A, rep row 2.

Rows 63–68: With A, rep rows 1 and 2 another 3 times.

Row 69: With B, rep row 13.

Row 70: With B, rep row 2.

Rows 71 and 72: With B, rep rows 1 and 2 once more.

Row 73: With C, rep row 13.

Row 74: With C, rep row 2.

Row 75: With B, rep row 13.

Row 76: With B, rep row 2.

Rows 77 and 78: With B, rep rows 1 and 2 once more.

Row 79: With A, rep row 13.

Row 80: With A, rep row 2.

Rows 81–90: With A, rep rows 1 and 2 another 5 times.

BO.

Back

With A, CO 72 sts.

Row 1 (RS): P5, *(K1 tbl, P1) 3 times, K1 tbl, P4, rep from * another 5 times, P1.

Row 2: K5, *(P1, K1 tbl) 3 times, P1, K6, rep from * another 5 times, K1.

Rows 3–90: Cont with A, rep rows 1 and 2.

BO.

Finishing

Hold front and back pieces with RS tog and CO rows at bottom. With tapestry needle and matching yarn, sew together with a backstitch along both sides and top edge, leaving lower edge open. Turn RS out. Insert pillow form and sew lower edges tog using overcast st.

CORNFLOWER PILLOW

Work same as the Mellow Yellow pillow, but switch the A and B colors and beg with B. Use cornflower blue for the back.

SAIL-AWAY PILLOW

Work same as the Mellow Yellow pillow, but switch the A and C colors and beg with C. Use white for the back.

WHITE SANDS PILLOW

Work same as the Mellow Yellow pillow, but switch the B and C colors and beg with A. Use cornmeal yellow for the back. As an alternative, make the back in the same stripe pattern as the front.

OCEANS PILLOW

Work same as the Mellow Yellow pillow, using alternate color choices as listed in "Materials" on page 69.

ROMANTIC RIPPLE VEST

Dress this feminine vest up or down. Wear it to the office over a dressy silk blouse or over a tee with jeans. The contemporary button closure makes the classic ripple pattern current. The model is made with a standard worsted-weight yarn, so it's easy to substitute other yarns.

Skill Level: Easy/Intermediate
Sizes: Small (Medium, Large)
Finished Chest: 36 (39, 41)"

MATERIALS

Galway from Plymouth Yarn Co. (100% wool; 210 yds; 100 g) in following amounts and colors: (4)

A	1 (2, 2) skeins of color 121 (light green)
B	2 (2, 3) skeins of color 15 (navy)
C	1 (1, 1) skein of color 98 (lavender)
D	1 (1, 1) skein of color 112 (beige)

- Size 8 (5 mm) circular needle, 29" long, or size to obtain gauge
- Size 8 (5 mm) circular needle, 40" long (for edging)
- Size 8 (5 mm) circular needle, 16" long (for armhole edgings)
- Size 8 double-pointed needles (for I-cord button loop)
- 2 large stitch holders
- 2 large decorative buttons, approximately 1" in diameter
- Sewing needle and matching thread
- Tapestry needle

TRY THIS!
Switch the blue and lavender sections, or change the navy to light blue for a summer look. Make it uniquely yours by using textured yarns instead of solids.

GAUGE

18 sts and 24 rows = 4" in St st

DIRECTIONS

Vest is worked in one piece to underarms. Cut yarn after each color use. Slip all sts pw.

Lower Section

Beg at lower edge with A and 29" circular needle, CO 244 (260, 276) sts and knit 2 rows.

BEGIN RIPPLE PATTERN:
Row 1 (RS): With A, K2, sl 1 pw, K1, psso, K5, *(K1f&b) twice, K5, sl 1 pw, K1, psso, K2tog, K5, rep from * another 13 (14, 15) times, (K1f&b) twice, K5, sl 1 pw, K1, psso, K2.

Row 2: Purl.

Rows 3–6: Rep rows 1 and 2 twice.

Row 7: With C, K2, sl 1 pw, K1, psso, K2, sl 1 pw, K2, *(K1f&b) twice, K2, sl 1 pw, K2, sl 1 pw, K1, psso, K2tog, K2, sl 1 pw, K2, rep from * another 13 (14, 15) times, (K1f&b) twice, K2, sl 1 pw, K2, sl 1 pw, K1, psso, K2.

Row 8: Purl.

Rows 9 and 10: With D, rep rows 1 and 2.

Rows 11 and 12: With C, rep rows 1 and 2.

Rows 13 and 14: With B, rep rows 7 and 8.

Rows 15–20: Cont with B, rep rows 1 and 2 another 3 times.

Rows 21–40: Rep rows 1–20.

Body

Row 1 (RS): Cont with B, K2, (sl 1, K1, psso, K1) 40 (42, 45) times, K1 (5, 9), (sl 1, K1, psso, K1) 40 (42, 45) times, K1—164 (176, 188) sts.

Row 2: Purl.

Row 3: Knit.

Row 4: Purl.

Rows 5–8: Rep rows 3 and 4.

Row 9: With C, K2 (4, 2), (sl 1, K7) 20 (21, 23) times, sl 1, K2 (4, 2).

Row 10: With C, purl.

Rows 11 and 12: With D, rep rows 3 and 4.

Rows 13 and 14: With C, rep rows 3 and 4.

Row 15: With A, rep row 9.

Row 16: With A, purl.

Rows 17–20: Cont with A, rep rows 3 and 4.

Rows 21–26: Rep rows 9–14.

Row 27: With B, rep row 9.

Row 28: With B, purl.

Rows 29–34: With B, rep rows 3 and 4 twice.

Rep rows 9–34 until piece measures 16".

Armhole and Shoulder

Continue in color and slip st patt as established.

Dividing row: Keeping to color and st patt, K37 (40, 43) for right front, BO 8 sts for underarm, K74 (80, 86) for back, BO 8 sts for underarm, K37 (40, 43) for left front. From opposite end of needle, place right front sts on one st holder, and back stitches on another st holder.

Left Front Shoulder and Neck

Beg on WS and keeping to color and slip st patt, work in St st for 2", ending on a WS row.

Next row (RS): Work in patt to last 3 sts, K2tog, K1.

Next row: Purl in patt across.

Rep last 2 rows until there are 19 (21, 23) sts on needle and armhole measures 7½ (8½, 8½)", ending on a RS row. BO.

Back

Slip back sts from holder onto needle. Keeping to color and slip st patt, work until back measures same as left front. BO.

Right Front Shoulder and Neck

Slip right front sts from holder onto needle. Beg on WS and keeping to color and slip st patt, work in St st for 2", ending on a WS row.

Next row (RS): K1, sl 1, K1, psso, work in patt across.

Next row: Purl in patt across.

Rep last 2 rows until armhole measures 7½ (8½, 8½)", ending on a RS row. BO.

FINISHING

Fold fronts to back with RS tog; sew shoulder seams. Turn RS out.

Edging

Hold vest with RS facing you; beg at lower right front edge in side of first row of body, with B and 40" circular needle, PU 2 sts for every 3 rows and 1 st along each BO st on back, adjusting sts so sts lie flat. BO. With 16" circular needle, work edging in same manner around each armhole.

I-Cord Button Loops

With B and dpns, CO 3 sts and move sts to opposite end of needle. Bring yarn behind sts on needle and beg with first CO st, K3. Do not turn.

Row 1 (RS): Slip sts to opposite end of dpn; bring yarn behind sts and K3. Do not turn.

Rep row 1 until I-cord measures 8". BO.

Sew buttons to center fronts at first B sections of body above ripple sections. Fold I-cord into a figure eight and tack at center to hold shape. Place loops over buttons; sew loop to vest on right front, leaving left front loop open. Weave in ends.

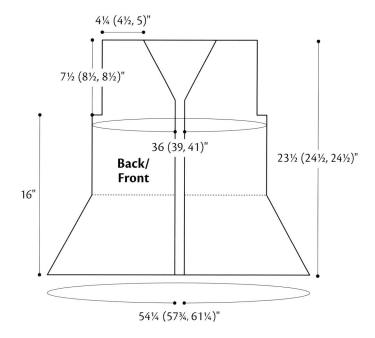

4¼ (4½, 5)"

7½ (8½, 8½)"

36 (39, 41)"

Back/ Front

23½ (24½, 24½)"

16"

54¼ (57¾, 61¼)"

PISTACHIO TEE

This summer top is designed for hot weather. The colors remind me of pistachio ice and strawberry ice cream.

Skill Level: Intermediate
Sizes: Small (Medium, Large)
Finished Bust: 34 (37, 40)"

MATERIALS

Meringue from Crystal Palace Yarns (40% merino wool, 40% acrylic, 20% elastic nylon; 123 yds, 114 m; 1.75 oz, 50 g) in following amounts and colors: (4)

- **A** 3 (3, 4) skeins of color 4103 Aloe
- **B** 3 (4, 4) skeins of color 0602 Vine-Green
- **C** 2 (2, 3) skeins of color 4891 Strawberry Cream

- Size 8 (5 mm) circular needle, 24" long, or size to obtain gauge
- Large stitch holder
- Tapestry needle

GAUGE

18 sts and 28 rows = 4" in St st with A

BACK AND FRONT (Make 2 identical pieces)

Note: For this project, I carried A along the side edges and cut B and C after each use. For tips on working with stripes in different yarns, see "Changing Colors and Carrying Yarns" on page 5 and decide which technique works best for you.

With A, CO 77 (83, 89) sts.

Rows 1 (RS)–3: With A, knit.

Row 4: With A, purl.

Row 5: With A, knit.

Row 6: With A, purl.

Rows 7 and 8: With B, knit.

Rows 9–12: With C, rep rows 5 and 6 twice.

Rows 13 and 14: With B, knit.

Rows 15 and 16: With A, rep rows 5 and 6.

Rows 17 and 18: With B, knit.

Rows 19 and 20: With C, rep rows 5 and 6.

Rows 21 and 22: With B, knit.

Waist Shaping

Row 1 (RS): With A, K1, K2tog tbl, knit to last 3 sts, K2tog, K1—75 (81, 87) sts.

Row 2: With A, purl.

Rows 3 and 4: With A, rep rows 1 and 2—73 (79, 85) sts.

Rows 5 and 6: With B, knit.

Rows 7 and 8: With C, rep rows 1 and 2—71 (77, 83) sts.

Row 9: With C, knit.

Row 10: With C, purl.

Rows 11 and 12: With B, knit.

Row 13: With A, K1f&b, knit to last 2 sts, K1f&b, K1—73 (79, 85) sts.

Row 14: With A, purl.

Rows 15 and 16: With B, knit.

Rows 17 and 18: With C, rep rows 13 and 14—75 (81, 87) sts.

Rows 19 and 20: With B, knit.

TRY THIS!

If you are more than a few years past your teens and want a more mature look, use off-white instead of pink. Now go out for strawberry ice cream!

Rows 21 and 22: With A, rep rows 13 and 14—77 (83, 89) sts.

Rows 23 and 24: With A, rep rows 9 and 10.

Rows 25 and 26: With B, knit.

Rows 27–30: With C, rep rows 9 and 10 twice.

Rows 31 and 32: With B, knit.

Rows 33 and 34: With A, rep rows 9 and 10.

Rows 35 and 36: With B, knit.

Rows 37 and 38: With C, rep rows 9 and 10.

Rows 39 and 40: With B, knit.

Beg with A, cont in stripe patt until piece measures about 9 (10, 11)", ending with 2 rows of B.

Cap Sleeves

Row 1 (RS): Cont in stripe patt, K1f&b, knit to last st, K1f&b—79 (85, 91) sts.

Row 2: Work in stripe patt.

Rows 3–6: Rep rows 1 and 2—83 (89, 95) sts.

Row 7: CO 2 sts onto RH needle, knit across, CO 2 sts—87 (93, 99) sts.

Row 8: Work in stripe patt.

Rows 9 and 10: Rep rows 7 and 8—91 (97, 103) sts.

Rows 11–24: Cont in stripe patt without inc.

Left Back/Right Front Shoulder and Neckline

Row 1 (RS): Cont in stripe patt, K38 (40, 42) sts, BO 15 (17, 19) sts, K38 (40, 42).

Row 2: Work in stripe patt across first 38 (40, 42) sts, place rem sts on st holder.

Row 3: K1, K2tog tbl, knit across—37 (39, 41) sts.

Row 4: Work in stripe patt.

Rows 5–16 (16, 18): Work rows 3 and 4 another 6 (6, 7) times—31 (33, 34) sts.

Cont in stripe patt until armhole measures 7½ (8, 8)" from beg of cap sleeve shaping, ending on a WS row. BO.

Right Back/Left Front Shoulder and Neckline

Place 38 (40, 42) sts from holder onto needle and hold with WS facing you. Cont in stripe patt, join corresponding color in first st and purl across.

Row 1 (RS): Knit to last 3 sts, K2tog, K1—37 (39, 41) sts.

Row 2: Work in stripe patt.

Rows 3–14 (14, 16): Work rows 1 and 2 another 6 (6, 7) times—31 (33, 34) sts.

Cont in stripe patt until right shoulder measures same as left shoulder. BO.

With RS tog, sew one shoulder seam.

Neck Edging

With A and WS facing you, PU 2 sts for every 3 rows along shoulder shaping and 1 st for each BO st on front and back, adjusting so sts lie flat.

Rows 1 (WS)–5: Knit.

BO on WS. Sew other shoulder seam.

Sleeve Edgings

Hold cap sleeve with RS facing you; with A, PU 2 sts for every 3 rows along edge of sleeve. Knit 3 rows. BO on WS. Sew underarm and side seams. Weave in ends.

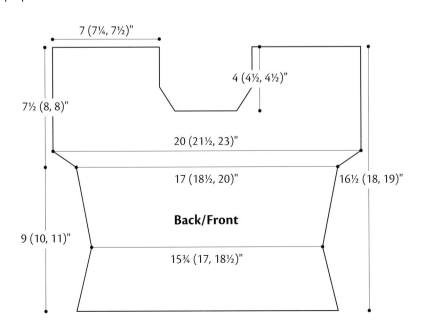

YARN RESOURCES

I wish to thank the following companies, who supplied the beautiful yarns used for the models in this book.

Cascade Yarns
PO Box 58168
Tukwila, WA 98138-1168
www.cascadeyarns.com

Crystal Palace Yarns
Straw into Gold, Inc.
Richmond, California
www.straw.com

Plymouth Yarn Company, Inc.
PO Box 28
Bristol, PA 19007
www.plymouthyarn.com

ACKNOWLEDGMENTS

Susie Adams Steele has been my model-making angel for so long, I can't count the number of projects she has created from my patterns. She knits better than most of us, with smooth, even stitches that speak to her many years spent as a knitter for St. John's Knits. I'm so glad she's now retired and working exclusively with me.

ABOUT THE AUTHOR

SANDY SCOVILLE has had a long career in needlework. After 13 years as a knit and crochet editor/designer for a major craft publisher and after seeing hundreds of her designs in print, she began writing her own books in 2001. A major contributor to the Martingale & Company Little Box series, she wrote three knit collections and coauthored five crochet collections with Denise Black. She has also created designs for several yarn companies.

Because her children and grandchildren live in other parts of the country, Sandy has found time to write three novels, be part owner of a small press, and work on a biography of her father and his love of San Diego and horse racing. She loves studying ancient and biblical history and, paradoxically, playing poker with friends every Thursday evening. She lives in San Diego County, California.